THE 7 CONNECTIONS TO HAPPINESS AND HARMONY

*Decision Making Made Easy
with Yoga's 7 Chakras*

By Shirley Desai

COPYRIGHT © 2009 By Shirley Desai

ALL RIGHTS RESERVED. No part of this book may be reproduced in any form or by any electronic or mechanical means including information storage and retrieval systems without permission in writing from the publisher, except by a reviewer who may quote brief passages in a review.

Editor: **James Hamilton**

Cover Layout and Illustration: **Lewis Agrell**

Desktop Publisher, Interior Pages: **Darlene Dion**

First Edition 2009

ISBN 0-9840613-0-4

Printed in the United States of America

Published by Shared Step Press

For Apurva

Table of Contents

My Journey:
Join Me on My Discovery of the Seven Chakras 1

Overview:
Application of the Seven Chakras in Decision Making 5

Chapter One:
The Root Chakra Connection – Safety and Fear 15

Chapter Two:
The Chakra Two Connection – Excitement, Pleasure, and Change 31

Chapter Three:
The Chakra Three Connection – Ego and Values 49

Chapter Four:
The Chakra Four Connection – The Heart Chakra 65

Chapter Five:
The Chakra Five Connection – Creativity and Self-Expression 83

Chapter Six:
The Chakra Six Connection – Analysis and Intuition 99

Chapter Seven:
The Crown Chakra Connection – Vision and Higher Purpose 113

Chapter Eight:
Bringing It All Together 127

Appendix 135

Acknowledgements 141

References 143

MY JOURNEY

Join Me on My Discovery of the Seven Chakras

Life can be a very challenging journey, during which we face many crucial decisions. At each juncture, we are confronted with important choices such as selecting a life partner, deciding on a career, moving to a new city, purchasing a home, divorcing a partner, planning for retirement, or fighting illnesses. While making these decisions, we are bombarded with thoughts in our minds and sensations in our bodies. When we are younger, many of these decisions are fun and exciting. But as years pass, the decisions seem to become more and more complicated.

In situations of high stakes or high uncertainty, the stress can feel overwhelming, impacting us on a mental, physical, or spiritual plane. Oftentimes, there is not one correct solution to a problem and we must decide between competing priorities. Ultimately, we want to make decisions that put us in a better position tomorrow than we are in today. We need to know that there is hope and happiness in the future and that we have the ability to find the answer that will lead us there.

In these high-stakes situations, our thinking can become constrained or clouded. Our moods, biases, and past experiences can color perceptions to such a great extent that we can make the wrong decision altogether. In addition, our fears and emotions can get the best of us. In effect, we are susceptible to reacting with our base instincts rather than according to our higher intellect.

The Secrets Behind Great Decisions

There are very important secrets to thinking and decision making. One secret is that we as humans have more potential than we realize for making great decisions. Within ourselves, we have the machinery and potential to access a wide assortment of information that can guide us in the best possible direction. Another secret is that as we tap this inner source, we discover a path to lasting happiness and fulfillment. The chakra system offers a comprehensive roadmap of human consciousness that brings together the physical, mental, and spiritual dimensions.

I stumbled across the chakra system through my study of Ayurveda and Hatha Yoga. The system of seven chakras is mainly associated with alternative healing modalities such as yoga, massage therapy, reiki, psychology, and gem therapy. For some people, much of this may be a bit too esoteric. However, as a business person learning about chakras, I found that the chakra system offered insight and clarity into other subject areas where understanding the thoughts, feelings, and motivations of people is important.

Ancient System Applied to Modern Life Challenges

This is not a typical book on chakras. A number of publications provide a specific, focused study of the chakras. The focus of this discussion is the application of chakras to thinking and decisions. In other words, how the chakras can help us find our best ideas and most fulfilling outcomes.

Greater Self-Awareness Leads to Better Decisions

The premise of my writing is that better decisions come from better understanding ourselves, in terms of both who we are on the inside and which processes we use in making decisions. This little amount of introspection can make our decisions fundamentally better, ultimately leading to more success and fulfillment.

In my workshops and discussions with people, some have related personal experiences with starting to understand their chakras. For these people, understanding came in surprising, unusual ways that felt empowering. My editor mentioned to me that as he read my manuscript, he began to analyze situations and thought processes from the standpoint of the chakras.

This book will provide an outline, chakra by chakra, of the various strengths and weaknesses we encounter in ourselves in making intelligent decisions. As we begin to connect with our inner chakras, we will begin to realize that within each of us, there is far more potential than we thought. In addition, we can begin to make decisions that ring true for us, that are balanced with who we are. Ultimately, we can lead ourselves to more happiness and success.

Looking at the chakras, we will discover that the first three are physically centered, dealing with our base needs as human beings. The three uppermost chakras are spiritually centered, focusing on our need for inner happiness and fulfillment. The fourth chakra is the bridge between these polarities. The best decisions are those that balance the practical needs of our life and society with our inner need for happiness and spiritual fulfillment.

Looking Ahead

The overview provides insight into the chakra system. Then, Chapters One to Seven take an in-depth look at the decision-making characteristics of each chakra, starting with the root chakra, all the way up to the crown chakra. Chapter Eight centers on how these chakras, taken together, can lead us to our best possible decisions.

There is a lot of information condensed in this small book, which I hope you will take time to read, re-read, and most importantly, reflect on.

 **THE 7 CONNECTIONS TO HAPPINESS AND HARMONY**

OVERVIEW

Application of the Seven Chakras in Decision Making

In my study of alternative healing treatments and principles, I was reminded that human beings have a physical body and an inner spiritual essence. The physical body is finite in all respects, with a set time of birth and time of death. Encapsulated in this finite body is our soul, which is infinite and timeless. Our soul is that unique vitality within us that defines who we are beyond space, time, or life form. Our minds connect these two worlds through the use of our seven chakras.

The Seven Chakras

The chakra system is an ancient physical, mental, and spiritual system that originated over 4,000 years ago in India. The term *chakra* stands for "wheel" or "disk" and is conceived of as a spinning sphere of activity that receives, processes, and expresses human life force energy. The life force energy is the energy that sustains life in our physical body. The chakras emanate from the major nerve centers that branch forward from the spinal column.

There are seven major chakras for human beings. Each chakra correlates to a region of the body or nerve center, which, in turn, correlates to levels of consciousness and spiritual and evolutionary constructs.

The 7 Connections to Happiness and Harmony

Chakra Seven
Vision and Higher Purpose

Chakra Six
Analysis and Intuition

Chakra Five
Creativity and Self-Expression

Chakra Four
Heart and Truth

Chakra Three
Ego and Values

Chakra Two
Excitement and Pleasure

Chakra One
Safety and Fear

The lower chakras (chakras one to three) correspond to our basic instincts and allow us to detect danger, sustain life, and enjoy earthly pleasures. I also refer to these as our base chakras or practical chakras. The higher chakras (chakras four–seven) relate to a more expanded intellectual state, allowing us to develop our higher powers of love, intelligence, creativity, intuition, and vision. The higher chakras help us gain more meaning and inner happiness.[1]

Early in my professional career, I made a concerted effort to suppress my inner voice. I tended to make decisions that made sense factually, regardless of what my inner voice was telling me, ultimately making some key mistakes. I learned the hard way that the inner voice should never be repressed. Rather, it is a valuable form of intelligence that should be developed. As I studied the seven chakras, the quality of information I received from my inner voice improved, as did the results of my related decisions.

According to the chakras, there is no magical line that can be drawn between rational thinking and emotion. Instead, there is a more logical method behind the mystique of thinking. Humans think, act, and make decisions based on a wider classification of thoughts, feelings, and emotions. Just as we have channels on a radio, we have channels of thought and feeling that guide us to act in a certain way:

- When we are scared, we act a certain way.
- When we are excited, we act a certain way.
- When we are angry or jealous or judgmental, we act a certain way.

Think about the different shifts in personality that someone close to you demostrates, based on the situations described here.

THE 7 CONNECTIONS TO HAPPINESS AND HARMONY

- When we have love or compassion, we act a certain way.
- When we analyze and use our intuition, we act a certain way.
- When we talk, communicate, or play instruments, we act a certain way.
- When we connect with our higher vision or purpose, we act a certain way.

Each of these classes of consciousness uses a unique set of intellectual and emotional "muscles." In other words, we carry around multiple behavioral tendencies that can be traced back to our energy centers.

The seven chakras stack in a column of energy originating at the base of the spine and radiating to the top of the head. Life force energy moves upward and downward on the spinal column and is processed through each of the seven chakras.[2]

One example of a significant discovery is Abraham Maslow's study of what he called "man's hierarchy of needs." His model was a pyramid with the base needs (roughly corresponding to the lower chakras) ascending to the loftier needs of self-actualization.[3] Since that time, other behaviorists have conducted additional studies to verify the link between emotions and human decision making. Superficially, if we compare Maslow's hierarchy of needs to the seven chakras, we see striking similarities among the categories and progression toward elevated thinking. However, there are also a few notable contrasts. According to Maslow's model, humans follow a sequential evolutionary path from basic survival to self-actualization in a step-wise fashion. With the seven chakras, there is both an upward and a downward flow of energy, and multiple chakras are in use at the same time. We engage in a balancing act to manage our needs across all of the chakras. For instance, a person who is under financial stress is still capable of connecting with his or her higher creative, intellectual, and spiritual self. In fact, this person is not only able to connect, but to juggle and balance all of these forces!

The Flow Energy from Chakra to Chakra

When talking about the chakras, it's necessary that we also address the flow or movement of energy between the chakras. The human life force energy moves like a two-way current (upward and downward) through two channel passageways.

Admittedly, I struggled for a long time to visualize the importance of the upward and downward movement of energy. Then recently, I realized that these upward and downward currents related to two unique modes of thought. There are two distinct outlooks or pulls in our thinking: **expansion** (in being open to information, people, ideas) and the opposite, **contraction** (in limiting information, reducing options, defining scope).

The upward current is the current of expansion, giving humans the energy to think more broadly, deeply, intelligently, creatively, and compassionately. The downward current is the opposing current, constricting thought to focus on physical survival, creating a mindset of limitations and practicality.

THE 7 CONNECTIONS TO HAPPINESS AND HARMONY

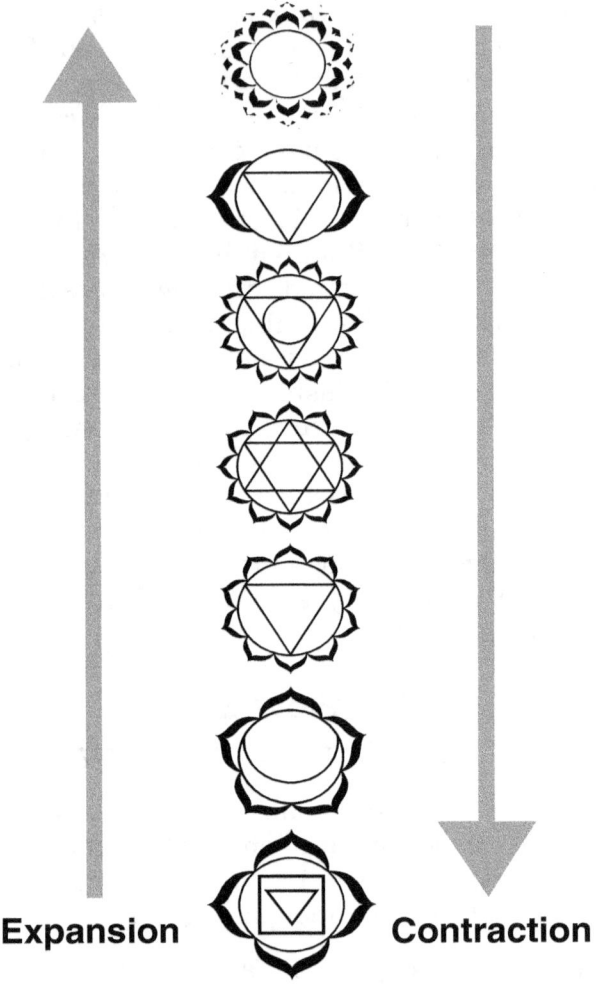

Expansion   **Contraction**

Blockages

Blockages result from over or under stimulation of a chakra, which impairs a person's ability to think clearly or fully. Each of these chakras has the potential to be overused (blocked), underused, or used in a healthy way. Each of us has certain blockages we carry with us. Some have blockages which relate to a particular political party (red state versus blue state). Some have blockages and prejudices based on organized religious beliefs (Christian, Jewish, Hindu, Muslim,

Buddhist, agnostic, or atheistic, etc.). When such blockages exist, they keep us mentally and emotionally stunted, unable to see the possible good and knowledge that we could process through our higher chakras.

While the majority of blockages exist at our lower chakras, there are also imbalances at our higher chakras; for instance, getting caught in a loop of analysis paralysis. When making important decisions, we should listen to all of our chakras but, ultimately, steer with our higher chakras, from a vantage point of calmness, clarity, and understanding. That is, allow our minds to play the role of orchestra conductor, leading us toward innovative thinking.

> **Can we accept criticism?** One example of remaining personally detached from positive and negative stimuli is in how we handle criticism. For most of us, at times, it can be difficult to accept criticism from others. But if we allow ourselves to accept feedback from others with a level of calm detachment, we not only become mentally stronger through criticisms, but also improve ourselves based on trusted feedback.

Chakras and Decision Making

The simple truth about the seven chakras in decision making is that each chakra provides an important dimension in our overall assessment of a situation. The chakras give us a lens through which

we look at the world. Collectively, these chakras work together to give us a feeling, or gut hunch, about the decisions we make.

As life circumstances change and as we evolve, our lens or outlook evolves. For example, when we are children, our desires may revolve around toys, candy, and attention from our parents. As we approach our teenage years, our attention may turn to shopping, music, sports, and any people who are not our parents! As we go through the inevitable ups and downs of adulthood, our priorities change. Therefore, we should make self-reflection an ongoing part of our decision process.

Challenges with the Decision Process

There is a significant challenge today in how people make decisions. When the stakes are high and where there is anxiety and fear, rather than thinking more creatively and clearly, people tend to constrain their flow of information. In effect, people draw their thought power from their lower chakras and operate at a level that is instinctive, reflexive, and reactive rather than proactive and thoughtful. However, we can reverse this tendency if we want to.

Mind – The Chief Gatekeeper

A fundamental principle of Yoga is that we, as infinite spirits, have infinite potential. In more specific terms, there is a very deep connection between mind and body, and the mind has influence over the body. There are known stories of Yogis and advanced students of Yoga who have successfully stopped their heart rate, walked on hot coals, miraculously healed illnesses, and much more.

For the non-Yogi, walking on hot coals is not yet an option! However, each of us has the ability to reframe our thinking by adopting a more fearless, creative, and positive mindset. For many, this means shifting from a tactical, reactive mindset to a strategic, proactive mindset. Our minds, as the orchestra conductor, will empower this shift if we allow it.

The Mountaintop Mindset

Mountaintop Thinking

The premise of any decision-making process should be to increase our flow of important information and ideas. An open mind and a broader perspective can open the floodgates to new ideas and opportunities that may have seemed unimaginable before. The mountaintop offers a beautiful metaphor for thinking. If we stand on top of a mountain, our clarity and insight will be far superior than when we stand at the mountain's foothills. The mountaintop mindset is one of calm control, in which we have access to vast information that is untainted by personal emotions and biases.

Our best decisions — whether selecting a university, a career, or even a spouse — are made when we remain open to both the possibilities and the pitfalls. The more we are attuned to opportunities, issues, challenges, and potential obstacles, the better our outcomes can be. For instance, a parent may not be willing to hear that his daughter or son is the one that is starting fights at school. A CEO may not want to hear that a product is inferior to that of the competition. But when it comes to decision making, an open mind can lead both the parent and CEO to the best outcome. Ignorance and closed thinking can lead to the wrong direction.

A Wide Range of Ways to Talk About Chakras

There is some variance in how the seven chakras are defined from publication to publication. In one source, certain traits or characteristics may fall in one chakra while in another publication, the same topics may be presented in a different chakra.

One reason for this is that the chakras are an ancient system spanning over 4,000 years, and they have been written about and revised even in the ancient texts. Over thousands of years, as one can imagine, many different ideas evolved. But also, the very nature of chakras is that they are vortexes of energy. Energy is a concept that is abstract to begin with and impossible to directly observe with the naked, untrained eye.

The 7 Connections to Happiness and Harmony

In addition, as a key underpinning of Yoga principles, our main device for understanding chakras is our own personal experience. The very nature of experiences is that each person has different experiences based on their unique personality and life circumstances.

Finally, as we step back and try to understand the specific role of each chakra, we must realize this will be an inherently challenging feat. This is simply because the seven chakras work together in an integrated, holistic fashion. It is much like cooking a soup: There are many ingredients that go into the dish, but at the dinner table, it will be hard to detect the individual ingredients.

If I Can Think It, I Can Achieve It

The final outcome is oftentimes the result of the right decision implemented correctly with the help of certain environmental forces. As with a game of darts, if a player focuses and aims properly and at the right velocity, she can hit the bull's eye. Once a decision is made, use strength, courage, conviction, and fearlessness to implement it. But our ultimate success lies in our vision. If we can think it, then we can achieve it.

With this overview in mind, we now look to each chakra one by one and examine how they relate to the process of making good decisions. After examining each chakra individually, we can observe how the chakras, taken together, can lead us to our best possible decisions.

In Summary

The seven chakras are seven intelligence centers which play a role in receiving and processing information to guide humans in decision making. The chakras correspond to classes of thoughts, feelings, and behavioral tendencies. The aim of any decision-making process should be to increase our flow of important information and ideas. Hence, it is important that we listen to all our chakras but decide in accordance with our highest intellect. With this background information, we begin an examination of the seven chakras as they relate to decision making.

CHAPTER ONE

The Root Chakra Connection
Safety and Fear

It All Starts with Fear

As we start out on our journey into our decision process, sometimes we can get stuck before we even get started. We aren't stuck because of a lack of information, vision, or interest. Sometimes, it is due to basic human fear.

Chakra One –
The Chakra of Survival

The *root* chakra is the first of the seven chakras. It processes stimuli and guides us in a direction that keeps us safe and secure. From the moment of birth there is a need for survival, a basic human instinct that is stimulated by fear and insecurity. For example, take an infant who begins to cry when his mother is out of sight. The infant is physically limited in his choices of expression or action. To that child, when mother is out of sight, there is no guarantee that she will return. To the infant, "out of sight" means "gone, possibly for good." Therefore, the child resorts to the activity that most often causes mother to reappear — crying.

The 7 Connections to Happiness and Harmony

As people mature, various levels of fear or insecurity must be dealt with. Fortunately, we have outgrown crying as our primary response to threatening situations. But our sense of threat and discomfort still continues to impact our sense of safety and balance — both in the life-threatening, catastrophic events like war and terrorism and in more benign situations, such as meeting new people. And our fears and insecurities play a significant role in many of the decisions we make.

Chakra One

Location:
At the base
of the spine

Sanskrit Name:
Muladhara

Color: Red [4]

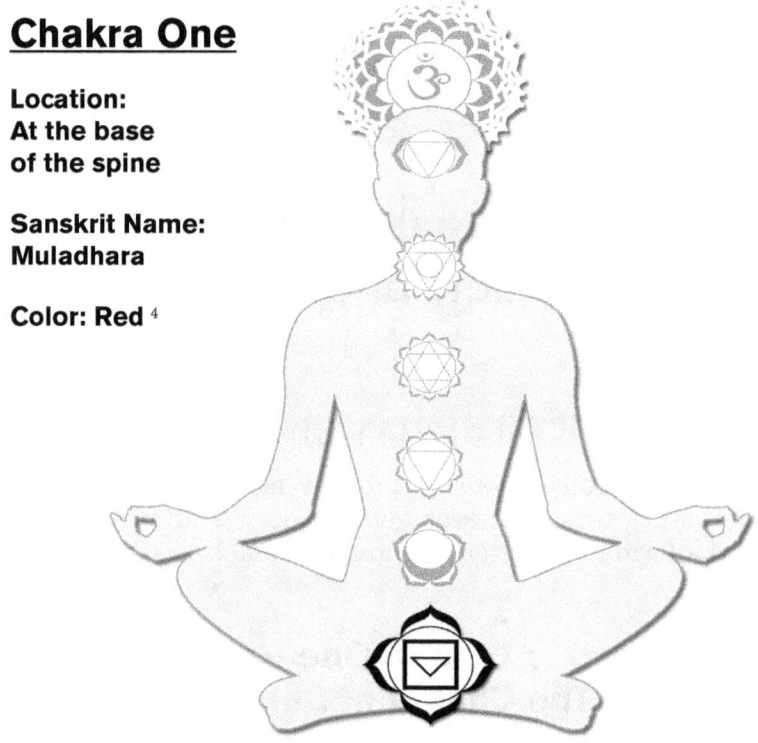

What Can Make Us Feel Safe?

Just like we don't want to walk into quicksand or venture into a black hole, the root chakra senses danger and uncertainty and navigates our decision making toward thoughts and actions that feel comfortable, stable, and less risky. We are almost magnetically drawn toward decisions that keep us connected to our families and social networks, decisions that make us feel safe, away from any kind of discomfort. This human characteristic may cause us to

Chapter One: The Root Chakra Connection – Safety and Fear

accept an unsatisfactory status quo or put off making decisions altogether. Each of us is born, socialized, and drawn to certain people, places, things, habits, and concepts that make us feel comfortable, secure, or at reduced risk. Whether a doctor who depends on available medical research or an obsessive-compulsive personality who cannot make a decision in a room where the carpet has not been vacuumed, each person will have his own criteria for determining his actions.

As discussed in Chapter One, each chakra is a vortex of energy that receives, processes, and expresses life force energy or decisions. The process of receiving, processing, and expressing can feel so natural that our thinking and our rationale for all decisions become instinctive chakra processes if we are not careful. But through establishing a mountaintop mindset, we can begin to decouple what we see and perceive from how we act. Below are a few examples of stimuli that we receive and process through our root chakra, which guides us in decision making.

Familiarity: Being in familiar surroundings where people do not face unexpected challenges eliminates the fear factor or, at least, relegates it so far into the background that only minimal caution need be exercised. For example, a person who has a dread of being in a crowd of strangers may be perfectly relaxed at a family reunion.

Roots: There is a connection to the soil where we live, whether it is our home, our city, our country, or the world at large. The entire nation of Americans, regardless of which part of the country they lived in, felt the attacks of 9/11 because it occurred on American soil. We are drawn to decisions that are linked to our roots.

Family Unit: There is security in marriage, children, and extended family relationships that is generally stronger than simply the bonds of common friendship. In most cases, it is family to whom people turn when difficulties arise. There is strength in the idea of group survival, the family working together as a single unit for the good of all. We are drawn to decisions that support our family unit.

Divorce and the Root Chakra
The impact of divorce can be significant because it impacts individuals and families at their very foundation.

Tribal Identity: As far back as our caveman ancestors, the familiarity of tribe or clan has been a mainstay of individual and unit security. The idea of strength in numbers, where the individuals are known and their reactions to various stimuli are reasonably predictable, creates a sense of security, lessening the impact of fear. Our tribal identity, nevertheless, can lead us down a path of faulty decision-making processes, such as herd behavior or groupthink. By falling into the trap of groupthink, we lead ourselves astray from our higher intellect.

> **Groupthink** is a type of thought exhibited by group members who try to minimize conflict and reach consensus without critically testing, analyzing, and evaluating ideas. Groupthink is a classic example of root chakra behavior.

Leaders and Authority: On a broader level, people find security in strong leadership. Religious people will look to priests, rabbis, gurus, or other spiritual leaders whom they trust to help them alleviate fears and insecurities. Students look to respected teachers and school administrators. Rank-and-file military personnel look to their commanding officers. Nations of people look to their elected leaders for security and safety. On and on the list might go, but these few should paint the picture of how people depend on leadership to help cope with fear. As in the situation of a somewhat dysfunctional family, people will accept various kinds of leadership because of the familiarity of the relationship.

Health: For many, good health is taken for granted, and no thought is put into preventative measures to prolong health until confronted with a serious health issue. Once people are confronted with a health risk, it can be a life-changing event as they focus on rectifying the illness.

Financial: Just the word *money* can set off a number of intense emotions. Some love money, some condemn others for loving money; nonetheless, money is a currency that makes people feel safe. So jobs and other aspects related to finances are fundamental aspects of living. You will notice that when a company is undergoing layoffs and people feel that their jobs are on the line, this causes a great deal of fear and anxiety. When we talk about finances and aspects of the root chakra, we find

CHAPTER ONE: THE ROOT CHAKRA CONNECTION – SAFETY AND FEAR

ourselves addressing not only purely basic needs but also one's lifestyle. In the modern industrial world, where the majority of the population has shelter and food, people are not as concerned with fulfilling basic needs as with fulfilling and maintaining a level of material comfort. Hence, financial concerns impact people of all economic brackets at their root chakra.

> **The Root Chakra and the Millionaire**
>
> Even for a millionaire who loses a part of his fortune, the loss and strain can feel destabilizing. In other words, it is not simply about basic living but also the attachments we have developed to our lifestyle.

Housing: Houses have become the reclusive place that gives one a sense of safety. Evidence of this desire for the security of home is the proliferation of businesses geared toward home improvement and the popularity of television shows featuring home design and decoration. Most recently, we have seen that the urge to own a home has led people to buy beyond their means with sub-prime loans they did not fully understand.

Mobility: We live in a mobile society, and the ability to drive a car or board a commercial airliner is a form of security for many people. Transportation keeps people connected to their tribes and families and employers. It has greatly changed our view on roots and distances, as we perceive the world to be smaller. Connectivity to our security centers is what makes our means of transportation so important.

Chakra One
Behaviors and Expressions

As mentioned above, we can see how chakra one can navigate us toward decisions and behaviors that seem safe and stable. From time to time, we are confronted with situations in which our safety is undermined. And this magnetic pull toward safety shifts into a fully focused response. At this point, let us consider some common ways in which chakra one behavior may manifest or express itself in humans:

The Fight or Flight Response

Once we find ourselves in an uncomfortable situation, when we

THE 7 CONNECTIONS TO HAPPINESS AND HARMONY

realize that we have stepped into quicksand, our fears and insecurities get stimulated to think and act in different ways. The "Fight or Flight Response," described by Neil F. Neimark, MD, identifies it in these terms: When we experience excessive stress — whether from internal worry or external circumstance — a bodily reaction is triggered called the "fight or flight" response.

Originally discovered by the Harvard physiologist Walter Cannon, this response is hardwired into our brains and represents a genetic wisdom designed to protect us from bodily harm. This response actually corresponds to an area of our brain called the hypothalamus, which, when stimulated, initiates a sequence of nerve cell firing and chemical release that prepares our body for either running or fighting.

In life-threatening situations, the fight or flight response helps to keep us safe.[5]

Overblown, however, the root chakra may cause us to panic or react in unacceptable ways, such as getting caught up in mass hysteria. We have all heard about how people have been trampled by others racing for the exits in a building fire.

Foolish Reactions

When we become afraid or insecure in our surroundings, there is often an immediate tendency to react to the fear in order to feel safe. Simply reacting to a fear may cause us to do very foolish things, like throwing water on a grease fire on the kitchen stove. In its most extreme form, the reaction might even be jumping out of a twenty-story office upon hearing that the stock market just crashed. Sudden fear may cause a

CHAPTER ONE: THE ROOT CHAKRA CONNECTION – SAFETY AND FEAR

perfectly innocent person to run when a policeman yells, "Halt!" It may also cause people to take their insecurities out on innocent bystanders or household pets.

> **The Old Woman Who Lived in a Shoe**
>
> You may recall the nursery rhyme about the "old woman who lived in a shoe and had so many children she didn't know what to do." Her fear was that of not being able to feed, clothe, and shelter the children; but her reaction was to "spank them all soundly and put them to bed," as if that would solve the problem.

Paralysis and Inaction

When we are shocked, fear may temporarily paralyze us. We have all seen movies where the heroine is standing frozen in her tracks as the monster begins breaking down the door. The audience begins screaming, "Run! Run!" but she just stands there, unable to move. Likewise, we have seen people walk up to a microphone in front of a crowd of people and then be unable to utter a word. Or maybe we have heard of someone in traffic who was unable to take his foot off the gas and slam on the brakes.

In much more benign situations, a milder form of this paralysis is shyness. We are out of the comfort zone of our core network, and the anxiety level may cause us to limit interaction due to fear or intimidation.

The Gnawing Sensation of Worry

The fear chakra's early warning system may manifest in a number of ways. Some common emotional responses include inertia, lack of sleep, anxiety, and continuous worry. For many, the feeling of worry or stress may include the physical sensation of a heavy weight on the chest region. Sometimes, worry can work like an infection that stays with us, causing us to obsess.[6]

As an almost textbook example, let me tell you about Ellen. She recently went through a period of great anxiety about her job security in an insurance office. Company profits were not as high as management wanted and a series of new people were sent to Ellen for training. She began having sleepless nights and sudden outbursts of emotion. She could not eat and had trouble expressing

THE 7 CONNECTIONS TO HAPPINESS AND HARMONY

herself in everyday conversation. It fortunately turned out that her job had never been in jeopardy. Instead, top management was planning to transfer her to a much larger branch within the company. Ellen's experience is not uncommon. The stress and fear of losing our livelihood is so devastating that it can wreak havoc on our ability to think rationally and calmly.

Handling Fear from the Mountaintop

As humans get scared, creativity and higher-faculty thinking can be compromised. And in the most extreme situations, behaviors can be completely out of whack from how a person normally operates. There is a landmark film, *Good Morning, Miss Dove*, which, while a fictitious story, exemplifies calm resolve and unconventional thinking used in a mountaintop mindset.

In the film, frantic depositors made a run on a small-town bank after the stock market crash of 1929. In the middle of the melee, Miss Dove, a respected schoolteacher, calmly deposited her salary. Former students of hers, seeing what she did, calmed down, and the bank was saved from ruin. Miss Dove's example allowed the small-town bank to make good on the cash the public had deposited there.

> **What are the types of behaviors and physiological sensations you experience when scared?**
> _____
> _____
> _____
> _____
> _____

Sometimes, during severe stress, people may even lose their ability to have coherent conversations. In the film, the disorderly clamor of frightened people was mitigated by the actions of a level-headed and well-respected woman. When

CHAPTER ONE: THE ROOT CHAKRA CONNECTION – SAFETY AND FEAR

the stakes are high, leaders need to stand tall, resilient, and calm in order to make the right decisions and inspire confidence in those looking to them for guidance.

Secrets to Mountaintop Thinking

The root chakra is the chakra where we can experience the most difficult obstacles in life. Given that our thinking can be hampered when having a root chakra experience, we must make an extra concerted effort to revitalize our thinking when confronted with a root chakra fear. There are ways to understand and think about fear when confronted with a challenging situation.

Say "No" to Fear

There is one secret to making smart decisions that is hidden under our noses and rarely taught in formal education. The secret is simply to *say "no" to fear*. We have convinced ourselves that as humans we do not have control over our thoughts and emotions and that we cannot control our fears. But surprisingly, saying "no" to fear is simpler than we realize. Coming back to the fundamental Yoga principles, they teach us that the mind has infinite potential. And while it may be difficult to harness or envision the idea of infinite potential, we do exercise mental willpower every day. Sometimes it is harder than other times, especially when we are staring at a delicious slice of chocolate cake! The chief challenge is that we do not want to let go of fear.

Over time, we have developed this attitude that fear is one of our defense mechanisms that keeps us in check. A little fear helps us along the way to maintain our health, finances, and relationships. Fear also helps us keep focus on the important, practical priorities of life. But there is a deeper question — do we want to operate through our fear center? Do we want to feel the anxiety of fear? Do we want to feel a sense of worry and that feeling of being out of control?

What if we shifted our mindset in favor of making decisions because they are the right thing to do, rather than because we are

scared? What if we operate from a mindset of making intelligent decisions and acting in accordance with the right answer? For a person considering the option of having an extramarital affair, what if he or she chose not to have an affair because it is the wrong thing morally and would hurt the spouse, rather than because of fear of getting caught? In other words, we do not need fear to be our motivator to take action. We can act in accordance with doing the right thing instead of in response to a fear. Should someone wait until there is a health risk to begin exercise and dieting? What if that person decided to act in accordance with the knowledge he or she had — that, just maybe, health risks could be prevented in the first place by staying in shape?

Letting Go of Fear

Fear is based on keeping attachments to people, objects, and ideas. But we must realize that all things in this life are temporary. Even if we attempt to latch onto permanence, we ultimately must give everything up at some point. At times, the world can feel like a cruel place. When we are young we feel immortal; as we age we realize just how finite our bodies and time are. The universe throws us curveballs in unexpected and mysterious ways. When these curveballs come to us, we have the choice of either latching on to our attachments with clinched fists or opening our fists and allowing nature to run its course. In other words, sometimes saying "no" to fear is not enough. We also have to completely let go of fear. When we open our fists and let go of fear, we open our minds to new possibilities that we may have never imagined before.

Take Pride in Failure

An old friend of mine grew up in a very rough neighborhood of Chicago. During his youth he became involved in a number of violent, physical fights. In reflecting on his experiences, he shared with me an interesting insight about fighting.

The person who has hit rock bottom is often more fearless than the person who has never been there. After all, he knows

CHAPTER ONE: THE ROOT CHAKRA CONNECTION – SAFETY AND FEAR

what the bottom has felt like. The idea is not to pick the wrong goals and be masochistic (so we continue to hit rock bottom) or to pick goals that are impractical or unrealistic. Rather, the idea is that we make intelligent choices but stay steadfast and focused on our goals in such a way that we don't allow ideas of fear or worry to creep into our periphery, undermining our ability to think clearly and creatively.

If a failure does happen, we can accept the failure and move on, pulling ourselves up from the wreckage and disappointment to chart a new course. This sort of resilience is what is needed in handling the up-and-down rollercoaster ride of life.

> *Success is the ability to go from one failure to another with no loss of enthusiasm.*
> — *Sir Winston Churchill (1874–1965)*

Shift from a Reactive to a Proactive Mindset

By the time we are faced with a threat or danger, it is often too late and will be expensive and hard to correct. As most medical professionals will agree, early detection is always key. Therefore, one can say that the best way to handle fear is to prevent a problem from taking root. Mountaintop mindset is not just one of fearlessness but also one of fear prevention.

We need our root chakra receptors to guide us in proactively sensing issues before they convert into problems. A proactive mindset is especially helpful in parenthood, in order to monitor and be attuned to potential pitfalls or challenges that one's children might experience.

In addition to being costly and difficult to handle, fearful situations cause our thinking to become constrained. Fear can inhibit or constrain the drawing of intelligence from our higher chakras. This leads to thoughts and actions which are more reactive than proactive.

Looking back at the story of Ellen and her fear of being made redundant at her office, there are some interesting observations.

Although she was picking up on the signals through her root chakra, she was also overcome with worry, limiting and paralyzing her capacity for fact finding and for communication with management. Ellen's fear would have served her well had she taken a proactive position rather than allowing the worry to get the best of her. In other words, her fear could actually have been her friend in the long run.

Take Smart, Courageous Action

Even with our wisest, most proactive decision, if our implementation is weak, the final result will be suboptimal and less effective. Only through a strong implementation can the strength of our vision and idea shine through. Therefore, once a thoughtful decision has been made, it's necessary to implement that decision with full courage and determination. The secret to courage is to be fearless once you have carefully, thoughtfully, and proactively arrived at a decision.

In talking with accomplished entrepreneurs in the Silicon Valley startup world, I have noticed a very interesting personality trait: their full confidence, optimism, and enthusiasm. While these successful entrepreneurs have faced many obstacles and continue to face challenges, they really possess the confidence in themselves and confidence in their vision to be successful. These entrepreneurs stay on top of the market and competition. However, they never allow fear, negativity, or doubt to enter their periphery.

At times, even with the most proactive mindset, we will be caught in situations where a threat to safety arises. The experience of fear is never a pleasant one. However, in some cases it can be our ally as an early warning signal of possible danger. It is analogous to a herd of antelope when one of the group senses danger and the entire herd takes off.

For the man whose fear for the life of his child causes him to rush into a burning building, there is no guarantee that either of them will emerge from the building alive. Nevertheless, taking a smart action is better than no action. It is comparable to the old saying that, "it's better to have loved and lost than never to have loved at all."

CHAPTER ONE: THE ROOT CHAKRA CONNECTION – SAFETY AND FEAR

Behind Fear Is a Golden Opportunity

The vast majority of human beings make important life decisions using a heavy dosage of their root chakra. The decisions that are made with help from the root chakra are not only safe decisions, but also ones which are conventional and which fit in with the norms of a group or community. Sometimes the golden opportunities arise when you begin to question assumptions, when you start to re-examine your personal definitions of fear, when you look for ways to simplify your fear chakra requirements.

The less baggage you carry in your fear chakra, the less you are tied down physically, mentally, and spiritually. You can start to see new ideas and new horizons which are completely opposite of what you imagined. Whether you want to work in foreign countries, start a business, or write your first novel, breaking down the door of fear can be your first step.

Begin with Baby Steps

Saying no to fear can be easier said than done, as our human connection and reaction to fear are hard-coded into our chakras and, of course, our biology. It is difficult and perhaps impossible to ever stop worrying cold turkey. (Ask any parent who still worries about their grown-up children.) But through baby steps, we can start to shift our outlook. And our ultimate goal will be to move from a place where fear controls our thinking to one where we are stronger, bolder, more resilient in the face of fear.

Baby Step #1

The first baby step is to be conscious of the fear and to make the decision to move past fear. We like to cling to fear because in a weird way, it gives us a feeling of instinctive comfort, it allows us to wallow, it allows us to not forget what we are afraid of. But rather than allowing worry to continue to grow and fester, the first step is to become aware of this fear and find ways to either contain the fear (so that it does not grow) and to look for a way to reduce its toll physically and emotionally.

Baby Step #2

When we are thrown into fearful situations, or situations of volatility and uncertainty, it is important to take a moment to breathe and find a way to relax. In yoga and meditation, there is this concept of finding one's center or inner calmness. And from this calmness, you can draw strength to evaluate options with a little more clarity and thoughtfulness than through simple reactive actions.

Baby Step #3

The third step is personal assurance or affirmation — wherever you draw faith, whether it is in a higher spiritual power, a specific religious faith, or in yourself — being able to say to yourself, "Things will be OK." Keeping that positive outlook is important.

Baby Step #4

Surround yourself with the right people. When we are stuck in a situation where we must make decisions and we don't know much about the choices, the situation can seem very dire, as in the case of terminal illness. What has helped my family is getting the feedback and advice of others and really trying to stay as open to different perspectives as possible.

Are there any fears that are holding you back?

_____
_____
_____
_____
_____

Baby Step #5

Fear gives us a notification of a threatening situation. However, fear itself can deplete our energy, keeping us less strong, sharp, and proactive in handling our fear. Use inner calmness to tackle problems proactively, effectively and with full determination.

In Summary

- The root chakra helps to steer us in our daily lives toward actions and decisions that make us feel safe, comfortable, connected to our social and geographic roots.

- The root chakra operates at our base instincts. This chakra helps us respond and be alert to our environment. However, it is not a place from which to draw intellectual or creative strength.

- When we are scared, the fear can sometimes stimulate irrational and foolish behaviors.

- Unaddressed fears can be immobilizing.

- Fear, as a friend, makes us attuned to risk and can motivate us to find a solution. We don't want to become mere reactors to fear or let fear control us. We need be attuned to our fears, think about the root causes, and proactively address them from that vantage point.

 **THE 7 CONNECTIONS TO HAPPINESS AND HARMONY**

Chapter Two

The Chakra Two Connection
Excitement, Pleasure, and Change

The Dynamic of Chakra Two

As we observed in Chapter One, the root chakra is focused on safety and security. Our tendency in the root chakra is to stay connected to our tribe, not to deviate — in a sense, staying the course. As we move to the second chakra, there is an added dimension that can seem quite the opposite. It is the one that gives us the impetus to make a *change*, to have *fun*, to *enjoy* a delicious slice of chocolate cake.

We can easily observe in the arena of politics how the first and second chakras may seem like competing currents. Many years prior to the landmark 2008 presidential election, a political strategist told me, "There are only two types of political campaigns. One is for staying the course and the other for making changes." The incumbent wants to continue things as they are (root chakra), but the opponent is all about making changes, taking action, finding excitement, and seeking pleasure — a second chakra appeal.

THE 7 CONNECTIONS TO HAPPINESS AND HARMONY

Chakra Two –
The Center of Excitement and Pleasure

The second chakra is multifaceted; it addresses movement, excitement, and sensory pleasure. In some literature, it has been classified as an irrational pull, as opposed to the more rational thought processes that emanate from the higher chakras. On the contrary, a better way of looking at chakra two is that it is an instinctive and natural part of the process of making important decisions and must not be overlooked. The most exciting decision may not be the best one; but at the same time, eliminating excitement and pleasure altogether is a recipe for boredom, blandness, or inaction.

Chakra Two

Location:
Lower abdomen

Sanskrit Name:
Svadhisthana

Color: Orange [7]

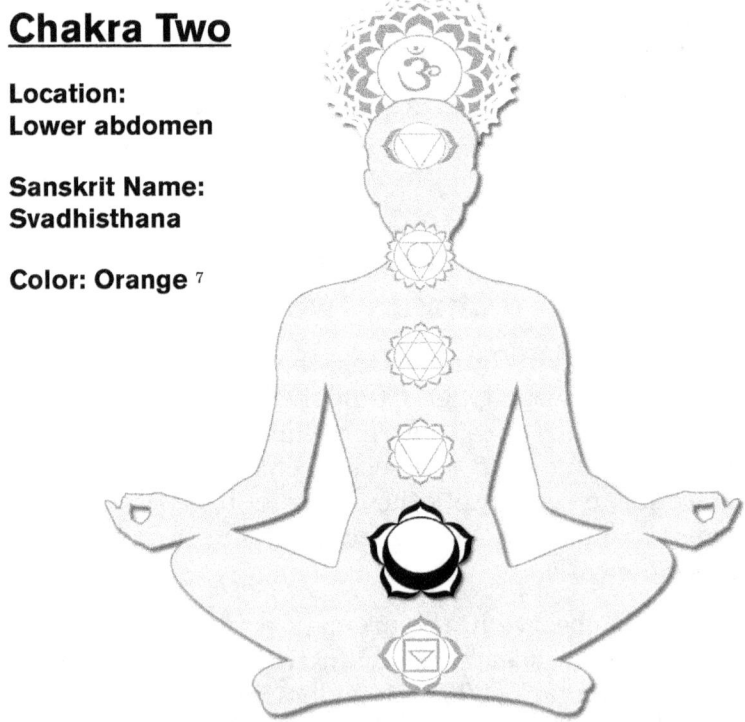

The second chakra is a key aspect in today's media. We can see how this plays out in the fascination with the beautiful people of Hollywood and the stars of cinema all over the world. Entire industries have sprung up centering on the lives and

Chapter Two: The Chakra Two Connection – Excitement, Pleasure, and Change

fortunes of the rich and famous. Rows of magazines at the supermarket checkout feature the faces of Angelina Jolie, Paris Hilton, Aishwarya Rai, and other glamorous stars, capitalizing on the public's fascination with celebrity.

In addition to physical attractiveness, the second chakra bolsters our sense of excitement and intrigue. It feeds off the energies of such diverse things as sporting events or conventions or exhibitions of the latest fads of gadgetry. It is the same satisfaction that keeps some of us glued to video technology and electronic games. Scalpers understand this principle, charging exorbitant prices for Super Bowl tickets. Large crowds turn out to see celebrities launch their clothing and fragrance lines. Shoppers become aggressive during a basement sale at Macy's.

Furthermore, since this chakra stimulates change, it serves as the impetus for diving into unexplored situations, a kind of sink-or-swim excitement that propels people into uncharted territory. From the sailing ships of the early explorers of the New World to the spaceships of modern-day astronauts, the second chakra centers on the emotional properties of excitement, change, and sensory pleasure.

Behavioral Tendencies in Chakra Two

On the positive side, chakra two behaviors include the participation and enjoyment of pleasures across the full tapestry of the human senses — allowing us to enjoy music, art, food, and the beautiful scent of flowers.

The buzz surrounding subjects of personal interest is another form of second chakra excitement. Marketers understand this characteristic of human nature and utilize it to promote products, people, and services. Sometimes the "buzz" manages to build momentum, as in the case of the J.K. Rowling Harry Potter novels. People actually camped out on the sidewalks to buy the next volume, making the books top the bestseller lists for a decade.

Intrigue is another stimulant that raises the excitement level; competitive games may satisfy the same needs. To gamblers, the thrill of the win is more important than the earnings. Cliffhanger sports raise the adrenalin levels of both the participants and the

spectators. Avid readers of mystery novels are caught up in the intrigue of the story and their attempts to solve the mystery before the final page.

> **What kinds of chakra two pleasures do you enjoy?**
> _____
> _____
> _____
> _____
> _____
> _____

New and different things or experiences are major factors in the level of the second chakra. The late Harish Johari, noted artist and author in Eastern spirituality, defines the second chakra person as one who "seeks occasions of amusement, visits clubs and parties, partakes in competitions, and seeks the attention of members of the opposite sex."[8] It is quite possible for anyone to recall anecdotal instances of operating at this second chakra level in daily life — bars and sporting events are full of them.

The strongest and most poignant example of second chakra pleasures is sexual gratification. The second chakra correlates to sexual and reproductive organs. For women, the desire for starting a family and motherhood can be traced back to the second chakra. As the desire to start a family is profound and instinctive, it goes far deeper than other desires or luxuries, all the way to our base, human fabric.

The Pull of Chakra Two in Decision Making

As we talked about in Chapter One, humans have an important, undeniable need to feel positive about decisions. The balance of positive must outweigh the balance of negative. Chakra two plays a pivotal role in decision making, providing

Chapter Two: The Chakra Two Connection – Excitement, Pleasure, and Change

that extra stimulation to jump into uncharted waters when making a decision. One example of this, is the mass appeal of the latest diet fad.

Different people find different things exciting or pleasurable based on their past experiences, unique personality, and current situation. As we look back on experiences we have had, whether traveling to new countries, trying new foods, or starting a business, chakra two can play an important role. If we didn't have the second chakra giving us that extra push, we may not ever try new things.

When we reflect on decisions, we will always think back to decisions that were positive and also decisions about which we ask ourselves, "What was I thinking?" Used in moderation, the pleasure chakra helps us make choices that will be personally satisfying. But we must also pay careful attention that second chakra influences do not impair or grossly contradict our better judgment.

Habits and Addictions

Habits have a unique role in chakra two to influence our thoughts, actions, and decisions. In our daily life, we carry around a number of good and bad habits that steer our actions. Certain habits or rituals, like daily bathing, are positive! Other habits, like watching hours of TV on the couch with a bag of potato chips, are less positive. Yet there are habits that offer a mix of both — like the morning coffee.

As we evaluate the role of daily habits, we see that good habits can keep us on the right path for making the right decisions for a more successful, fulfilling life. Yet certain habits can keep our consciousness centered around chakra two gratifications. On one level, this can inhibit our ability to focus and concentrate. (If our mind is focused on coffee, we may not allow ourselves to function fully without it.) Taken to the extreme, as in the case of politicians and sexual misconduct, one's mind gets so stunted by chakra two narcissism that it results in complete laxity or failure in judgment.

Classically, failures in judgment can be seen in sexual scandals

THE 7 CONNECTIONS TO HAPPINESS AND HARMONY

with elected officials at every level of government. While it would be far too simplistic to suggest that we can attribute such large lapses in judgment to a single chakra, we can definitely make the case that in giving in to the urge for chakra two gratification (and chakras one and three also), these politicians did not take into account the more rational, spiritual, ethical, emotional aspects of the higher chakras. It's highly unlikely that a politician conducted a focus group to assess whether a scandal could be accepted by his voters before making the disastrous decision! Giving in to the base chakras dominates higher thinking and weighing the potential risks associated with the dignity of the office, sanctity of the family, and public opinion of the voters.

Are there any habits that you would like to change?

In the most devastating scenarios, chakra two excesses can lead to addictions that are destructive for the individuals and their families. Intellectually and spiritually, these addictions impede the progress of the individual. For example:

- Compulsive gambling bases thought on the next chance of hitting the jackpot.
- Alcoholism or drug addiction focuses thought on the next drink or fix.
- Compulsive shopping limits thought to the sensory gratification of finding the next bargain and making the purchase.
- Overeating causes people to go to extremes with food.

CHAPTER TWO: THE CHAKRA TWO CONNECTION – EXCITEMENT, PLEASURE, AND CHANGE

There are brilliant thinkers and famous entertainers who have fallen into the trap of dangerous addictions, which ultimately lead to their demise. People caught in the loop of merely satisfying sensory experiences are incapable of thinking beyond their compulsive responses on that level. Entire systems of treatment and rehabilitation have been developed to deal with such blockages.

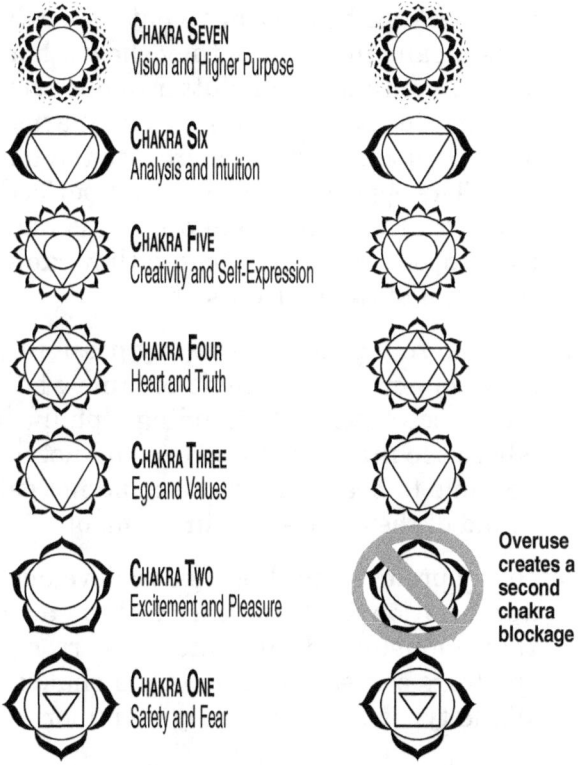

Overuse creates a second chakra blockage

Sensory Blockage of the Second Chakra

In addition to habits and addictions, there are wholly different forms of chakra two blockages. This is associated with imbalances we feel with our senses. For example, there are any number of external things that bother us to the point that we cannot concentrate on anything else.

- Particular odors become blockages for some people. Foul smells, for example, may often completely eliminate the

desire for food. In Asia, for example, there is a fruit called the durian which is said to have a very pleasant taste. Many people, however, refuse to try it because the fruit has a most disagreeable smell.

- Clutter for some people can be a factor that shuts down any kind of mental process. Realtors recognize this blockage by creating what they call "staging." This means that before they show a house, they have the sellers remove all clutter and create a setting that evokes beauty and a pleasant atmosphere. The staged setting actually increases the likelihood of a sale. The opposite is also true. A perfectly wonderful house that is cluttered and filthy is likely to turn off the prospective buyers before they can see the true potential of the house itself.

- Certain sounds may block any possibility of gratifying a sensory craving. A friend of mine who has perfect pitch once described attending a philharmonic concert where the flute was flat. He could not enjoy the music he came to hear because he could not get past the sound of the out-of-tune instrument.

- In my professional life, I have developed a keen appreciation for "spell check." I am acutely aware that publishing documents with errors and misspellings can easily stimulate a chakra two blockage. While typos might actually be minor to the author,

> These blockages may occur because of distracting externals that tend to shut down any possibility of experience at all. Research indicates that more people than one might think are highly susceptible or sensitive to stimuli. In her book, *The Highly Sensitive Person*, Dr. Elaine Aron states that being highly sensitive affects fifteen to twenty percent of the population. Furthermore, highly sensitive people are easily over-stimulated, which might lead to a range of blocking emotions such as rage, being overwhelmed, or frustration. This has recently opened up an entire field of study to determine psychological methods of helping highly sensitive people survive.[9]

Chapter Two: The Chakra Two Connection – Excitement, Pleasure, and Change

the impact to readers is significant. Ultimately, these blockages can easily detract from the value and essence that is conveyed. Hopefully, you can overlook any errors you might find within this book!

Industry Focus on Chakra Two

Undoubtedly, because of the emotional power of the second chakra, entire industries have grown up to take advantage of this powerful motivating force within human beings. Las Vegas, Hollywood, and Toys "R" Us™ are examples that come quickly to mind. Children operate largely from this level — a fact that is observable when children are shopping with their parents in the supermarket. One can watch children grabbing items off the shelves that appeal to them through color of packaging or the promise of fulfilling some personal gratification. For the most part, children will spot the sugar-coated cereals and cartoon celebrity-endorsed confections. It is unlikely that one ever sees children running for the broccoli.

Recently, the marketing of unhealthy sugar-laden products during prime times for children's television programming — Saturday cartoons and after-school children's programs — has come under fire. The backlash from parents against such practices has caused many companies to pull their ads during those viewing times. The efforts to moderate children's exposure to advertising that appeals to their sensory level, however, have still not motivated children to run to the broccoli displays in the supermarkets.

Certainly, the movie industry is focused on providing chakra two gratification. If people did not become excited, emotionally involved, and immersed in the special effects in cinema, it would not be the major industry we observe today. Television, from the entertainment shows to the news, also provides chakra two stimulation. An entertainment trend of the last decade has been the so-called reality shows that allow viewers to participate vicariously in a high-stakes, cutthroat competition offering a complete change from modern suburbia. In fact, television ratings and movie box office receipts hang largely on the chakra two sensory appeal to audiences. Even newscasts, which were once delivered by middle-aged, somber men, are now being presented by an assortment of very attractive and articulate females.

The 7 Connections to Happiness and Harmony

"If you put a crouton on your sundae instead of a cherry, it counts as a salad."

Other industries that involve the arts fall into this same category. Museums, concerts, and poetry readings are examples of commercial events that stimulate the chakra two need for gratification. Travel is another activity that incorporates change and excitement. Travel agencies, airlines, and cruise ship lines center their advertising around new and exotic places to visit as well as the attractive people on board.

In recent years, surprising industries have sprung up to feed off the second chakra focus on physical attractiveness and desirability. Dentistry, which was formerly thought of with the same dread one associated with torture chambers, has become a purveyor of whiter, straighter, and more beautiful teeth. Surgery, done for cosmetic reasons as opposed to only life-saving necessity, is now glamorized on syndicated television shows. Balding men are bombarded with assurances that they can restore their natural hair and suddenly live a more exciting life by looking more attractive. Skincare, anti-aging creams and lotions, fad diet programs, and concealing

CHAPTER TWO: THE CHAKRA TWO CONNECTION – EXCITEMENT, PLEASURE, AND CHANGE

cosmetics for both women and men are other industries aimed at people operating at the chakra two level.

The Monotone Professor

Sitting in a lecture hall listening to someone drone on and on about some required subject for a major degree will most likely not stimulate the second chakra. Such situations are generally labeled "boring" and only perpetrate a certain ennui. In contrast to that, fifty-yard-line seats at the Rose Bowl or Super Bowl stimulate the excitement chakra in avid sports fans.

Mundane exchanges of conversation may not be stimulating, whereas salacious rumors, for many people, stimulate the excitement of prurient interest — ergo, the success of scandal magazines and shock jock radio. Different people, of course, respond differently to various stimuli. For example, the person whose passion is symphonic music will experience second chakra excitement at the New York Philharmonic, whereas an avid rap fan would be as bored as the student sitting in the required course lecture hall.

Marketing to Chakra Two

The aim of advertisers is to appeal to the second chakra for creating pleasure and excitement to encourage trial. Design firms and packaged goods companies have become masters in creating an integrated brand experience. The whole idea of a "brand experience" is based on appeals to the five senses. Take the look and feel of driving a brand new Mercedes™, for example. Carefully crafted advertisements aim toward giving the viewers a sense of actually sitting behind the wheel, smelling the scent of new car leather, smooth drive, and excellent acceleration.

In today's society, the mere mention of the name Starbucks™ conjures up the aroma of a favorite coffee. In terms of satisfying one's chakra two desires, the experience of simply entering the Starbucks shop is almost as satisfying as the taste of the drink one orders there. The interior is upscale, the coffee aromas permeate the room, and contemporary music plays in the background. While in the early days Starbucks was a status symbol, with its spread into nearly every major town and with drive-through Starbucks in

THE 7 CONNECTIONS TO HAPPINESS AND HARMONY

many locations, the brand cache or exclusiveness has diminished to a certain extent. But in exchange, Starbucks has become the official currency for quality coffee and related drinks.

Pleasure from the Mountaintop

As we ponder thinking and decision making, the role of chakra two can seem puzzling at times. We know that chakra two does not really lead us to decisions that are smart or intellectual, yet it does lead us to decisions that make life enjoyable, give us something positive or tangible to look forward to, especially in the short term. How do we reconcile the needs of sensory pleasure with the needs for intelligent decisions? For the person who wants to travel the world versus going to medical school, how does he or she reconcile the short-term pleasure with the longer-term benefit?

The simple answer is that each chakra corresponds to important dimensions of life. And second chakra pleasures are one important dimension. The second chakra provides an important link with the world around us, allowing us to stay more aware and grounded. The working mother who is constantly juggling responsibilities has limited time to take care of herself. However, maintaining balance as a person is critical for clear thinking and effective decision making. Thus, maintaining a moderate use of chakra two is valuable for all of us in keeping an overall balanced mindset.

However, as we make important decisions, we should also realize that short-term pleasures do not equate to long-term happiness. As human beings and infinite spirits, we have the potential to realize lasting fulfillment and happiness. Happiness begins at chakra two, with temporary sensory gratification, but deepens as we connect more deeply with our higher chakras. And as we make decisions, we should look at those options that keep us balanced and fulfilled and also that lead us to a vastly greater plane of fulfillment.

CHAPTER TWO: THE CHAKRA TWO CONNECTION – EXCITEMENT, PLEASURE, AND CHANGE

Secrets to Utilizing the Base Chakras for Mountaintop Thinking

Mountaintop Thinking

▲▲ **Don't Judge a Book by Your Second Chakra**

Today more than ever before, packaging has evolved to an art form, designed to appeal to the centers of emotional and sensory satisfaction. The packaging of products and people suggest that we will find excitement, amusement, change, or sensory gratification in the products or personalities. Viewed only from the second chakra level, potential leaders may come across as political panaceas when, in fact, if viewed through all seven chakras, they would not even make the cut. Certainly Hollywood for years persuaded us that this star or that one is "the most beautiful woman in the world." In other words, it requires looking for the inner essence that is often veiled by the packaging and hype.

By looking for the goodness that lies underneath the surface, we can spot that diamond in the rough. Take, for example, a dilapidated house that could be picked up for a song, but sensory-level thinking passes it by. It is quite possible that someone else might view it differently, seeing the potential for fixing it up and flipping it for a good profit. It gives such a person a distinct advantage to be able to see beyond the level of immediate gratification. By careful examination and consideration, many people find the real winners that have been well disguised by chakra two blockages!

▲▲ **More Does Not Mean Better**

In Western culture, there is a mantra of "more is better," which is splattered across media programs and their sponsors, the advertisers. There is a heavy emphasis on material, external factors in defining inner happiness. Whether driving a certain type of car, owning multiple houses, marrying the most beautiful woman, or purchasing the latest electronics, the outer comforts become the defining traits of happiness.

Scientifically, research has shown that repeated indulgences lose their appeal. Scientists call this process habituation or adaptation, a condition that is observable in everyone. The first taste of some new and satisfying flavor creates a pleasure that is never again recaptured.

THE 7 CONNECTIONS TO HAPPINESS AND HARMONY

There are some natural limitations to pure sensory and material pleasures, as they will be fleeting. We reach a natural saturation point in our ability to enjoy pleasure. Even beautiful music, if we hear the same piece too many times, can start to become less appealing and sometimes even be annoying. Holiday music when it is first played in the malls may excite us, but after so many renditions of "Jingle Bells," the music begins to grate on the nerves. While we can find new interests to keep ourselves occupied, over time, we will at some point get bored. At which point, we begin to seek pleasures that are more rewarding, timeless, and infinite — our higher pleasures.[10]

▲▲ Seek Higher Pleasures

Martin E.P. Seligman, an American psychologist, discusses the very important topic of happiness in his breakthrough work in positive psychology, *Authentic Happiness*. He defines pleasures as producing "raw feels" that include such things as "ecstasy, delight, mirth, exuberance, orgasm, and comfort."

As we look at what the positive psychologists have uncovered in their research, we see a direct tie to chakras. Mihaly Csikszentmihalyi, professor of social science at the Peter Drucker School of Business at Claremont University, talks about a "flow," which he describes as a "state of gratification when we feel completely engaged" in an activity. Whatever that may be for different individuals, he notes that it produces a feeling of "time stopping" for the person involved. In these higher pleasures, the individual is challenged, concentrates, and has clear goals in mind, and the sense of self diminishes.[11]

In simple terms, we should not limit or constrain our view of pleasure to activities that stimulate our physical senses. Through the use of our higher faculties, we can develop a more satisfying experience. So instead of watching a television show, someone may derive significantly more pleasure in running a marathon, finding a cure for cancer, or writing a novel. In chakra two, as we look to become happier in our lives, we can add new activities that give us more personal gratification — moving us from thinking

CHAPTER TWO: THE CHAKRA TWO CONNECTION – EXCITEMENT, PLEASURE, AND CHANGE

about happiness only in terms of sensory pleasures to thinking in terms of higher pleasures. In other words, as we think about higher pleasures, we should look at our higher chakras.

Martin Seligman outlines specific character strengths and virtues that lead to happiness in *Authentic Happiness*. His book offers a formula that directs our thoughts and behavior from just the sensory pleasures toward our higher capabilities for a more fulfilling life experience. The relatively new movement of positive psychology is an encouraging step toward empowering people to expand mentally, physically, and spiritually for a happy and fulfilling life. While the character strengths and virtues that Seligman outlines do not directly map to the seven chakras, there is quite a natural correlation. The virtues he speaks of correspond to higher chakra experiences. The more we focus on activities and actions that stimulate our higher chakras, the happier we are. And ultimately, as we get more comfortable with our higher chakras, the greater our potential becomes to learn, think, and make wise decisions.

> **Can you think of any activities during which you experience an enjoyable feeling of time stopping?**
> _____
> _____
> _____
> _____
> _____
> _____

▲▲ Simple Living and Higher Chakra Thinking

I used to believe that those who consciously chose a life of simplicity were choosing a life that was bland. But as I started to get more immersed in my creative passions, I realized that simple living is far from boring. It actually means living a life that is rich in passion. Simple living means that we limit our desires for material possessions so we can redirect our time, energy, and emotions to our passions and pursuits.

The 7 Connections to Happiness and Harmony

By saying simple living, I am not suggesting that it is immoral to enjoy nice things or that as humans we should not have material desires. Material pleasures do bring a valuable dimension to the world that makes us enjoy and appreciate the splendor of the world. And consumption of products supports a global economy. But in our pursuit for physical pleasures, we should realize that these pleasures do not buy lasting happiness. This is because happiness comes from within.

That is why I say that in addition to our physical happiness at chakra two, focusing on finding happiness in our inner self or spirit can guide us on a path of making the choices and tradeoffs in favor of personal passion and meaning.

Mountaintop Thinking

A Motivational Checklist for Mountaintop Thinking

1. From the mountaintop, we can start to reframe our thinking to look beyond base pleasures toward pleasures that extend beyond our basic, instinctive needs. We can start to rethink pleasures as activities that feed our soul, that give us meaning, that allow us to expand our personal capabilities, that fire our human passion.

2. Igniting chakra two for action and change is the first big step in motivating people.

3. Moderating chakra two will prevent us from making those superficial decisions based solely on appearances, which often give us a false sense of reality.

In Summary

- Similar to chakra one, chakra two is a more instinctive center that addresses movement, excitement, and sensory pleasure. Chakra two allows humans to enjoy such experiences as travel, music, food, wine, and sports.

CHAPTER TWO: THE CHAKRA TWO CONNECTION – EXCITEMENT, PLEASURE, AND CHANGE

- Thinking at chakra two may cause us actually to miss out on some wonderful opportunities simply because there is no immediate buzz or sensory pleasure around them. We might overlook a profession that is actually thrilling work, or we may not visit a place that offers stimulating vistas and activities.

- Underuse of the chakra can make us out of touch with the world. This is comparable to the absent-minded professor who is so wrapped up in his field that he simply cannot connect with his students. We need to spend quality time with others to keep ourselves linked up to the world.

- Chakra two in moderation allows us to make the most balanced decisions.

**THE 7 CONNECTIONS TO HAPPINESS AND HARMONY**

CHAPTER THREE

The Chakra Three Connection
Ego and Values

Up until now, with chakras one and two, we have talked about factors that are more instinctive, the energies that keep us safe, the energy that motivates change. Now we move to the energy that uniquely defines self, our sense of right and of wrong, and the actions we do that are in accordance with our beliefs. At this point, it is possible to begin seeing how the chakras build upon one another in a constant connection of energy that we picture as running up and down the spine.

In Chapter Two, we observed the sensory chakra that drives the needs of personal gratification and excitement, which include the elation of change. In infants these stages are acutely observable, possibly because of the fact that from the time we are born, each chakra is in the development stage. First, the infant is concerned only with survival, demanding to be fed and exhibiting insecurities by its only means of communication — crying. As the infant gets older, it begins to develop its sensory identification. The child demands to be entertained. The search for sensory gratification is on.

Now we turn our attention to the third chakra, which involves

THE 7 CONNECTIONS TO HAPPINESS AND HARMONY

the *ego and self-definition*. Again, this is acutely observable in children, as they enter what some have called the terrible twos. At this stage in their development, children begin to push the envelope, to test the boundaries of what they can do and how far they can go with various behaviors. The child is developing his or her own sense of self and autonomy. In this phase, the individual differences between children — even siblings — is more noticeable. More distinct personality develops as the child becomes more action oriented and begins to learn a sense of right and wrong.

The third chakra is our personal power center, from which we draw our self-image. Physically, this center controls our metabolism and, when healthy, provides energy, effectiveness, spontaneity, and non-dominating values of the ego. In other words, at the core of all human beings is a soul that is virtuous and good, that wants to do the right thing. Used correctly, chakra three applies these sterling qualities to our decision-making processes.

Chakra Three

Location:
Solar Plexus

Sanskrit Name:
Manipura

Color: Yellow [12]

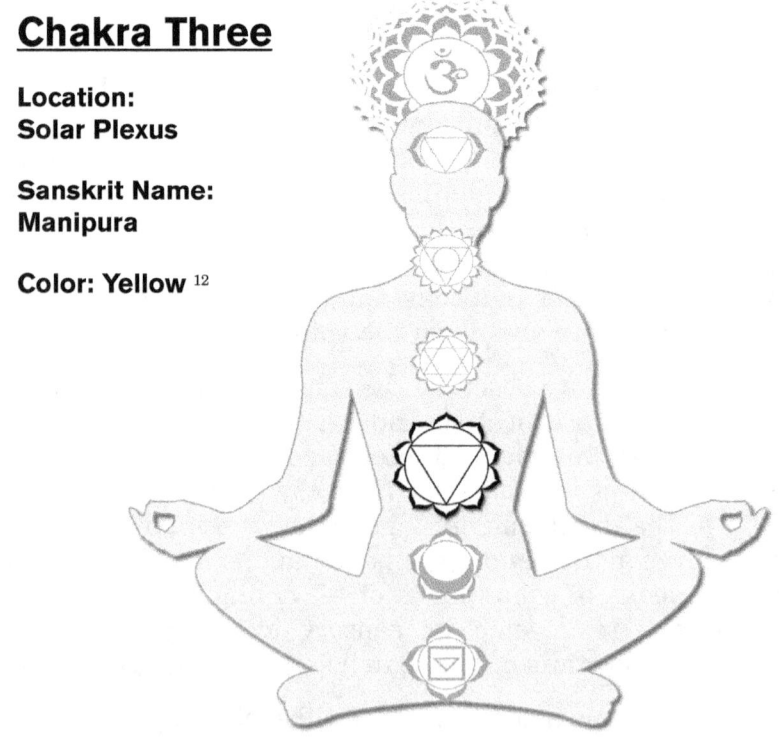

CHAPTER THREE: THE CHAKRA THREE CONNECTION – EGO AND VALUES

Chakra Three by Definition

The word *ego* may be defined from several vantage points. *The American Heritage Dictionary* defines *ego* as "the self, especially as distinct from the world and other selves."[13]

In philosophy, the term signifies the self as distinct from the outside world or other selves. In the area of psychoanalysis, the ego is defined as that part of the mind containing consciousness. In negative terms, ego is considered to be an over-inflated estimation of one's value. The word ego can conjure up a lot of images and ideas.

For instance, when women talk about the "male ego," it is usually in reference to men's attitudes, such as not stopping to ask for directions when driving in a strange place. Of course, the ego is not limited to males as this is a trait of all humans. Colin Powell described the role of ego in decision making when he said, "Look for intelligence and judgment and, most critically, a capacity to anticipate, to see around corners. Also look for loyalty, integrity, a high energy drive, a balanced ego and the drive to get things done.[14] It is that balance of the third chakra, together with the other six, that we are looking for in our quest for better decisions.

By any definition, the ego of chakra three is that image formed of oneself, self-identification, distinctive recognition of the self, and the level of perceived power of the self. Reputation is a primary concern at chakra three, in many cases driving the ego toward name and fame. Chakra three individuals are mainly concerned about personal authority and social status.

> **What are the organizations, roles, ideas, or groups that you identify with?**
>
> _____
> _____
> _____
> _____

Ego – An Impediment to Mountaintop Thinking

The ego, or sense of self, is oftentimes an attribute of high achievers and highly successful individuals. Certain fields attract individuals with large egos. There is naturally a need to have a balanced ego. But once the ego becomes excessive, many problems and obstacles can arise. By taking on behaviors that overstimulate our egos, we may perceive ourselves as invincible and righteous, pulling us away in directions counterproductive to desired goals.

Therefore, it's important to realize that an imbalance in our ego can actually produce counterproductive results. The reason is that as the ego gets more involved, we lose sight of the higher goal, the higher mission, and we focus on activities that stimulate our self-worth. In the more extreme cases, the entire effort or strategy becomes focused on fulfilling, demonstrating, or defending one's self worth. We see that this ego chakra can affect organizations, nations, ethnicities, castes, or institutions where the leaders and members bestow a feeling of power and superiority. This self-worth can at times demonize the opposing viewpoint. There are certain examples of ego behaviors:

- **The Bully** is a prime example of the ego out of control. From the schoolyard intimidator to the office tyrant, this type of personality has a sense of superiority and of the right to have everything his or her way. Even the bully, however, seldom thinks of himself as a "bad person." There is that element of the ego that has a basic desire to feel good about one's self-concept. In the case of the bully, the concept is distorted by self-interest.

  A large man may see himself as so physically powerful that he can do whatever he pleases with impunity. He is, in a way, the 800-pound gorilla. He is forceful and aggressive. In any situation, this man commands

CHAPTER THREE: THE CHAKRA THREE CONNECTION – EGO AND VALUES

center stage and control, which he views as an inalienable right. We might run across him in the office, where his insatiable need for power and control completely dominates the workforce. In a domestic situation, he is the overbearing and dominant partner or parent. People who have such a drive for power possess an extremely active third chakra.

- **The Chest-Thumping CEO** probably sees himself or herself as an astute business person. Inevitably, however, the actions of such a person, whether in hardnosed business dealings or in dictatorial stances toward the employees, are motivated by personal aggrandizement. The motivation behind such behavior is to make oneself look good. Certain ego-minded CEOs will make decisions based on image and status of self or the ego he or she attaches to the company, rather than in the best interest of employees or shareholders.

- **The Egomaniac** has an overblown sense of self-worth. Possibly everyone has read at one time or another about famous film actors whose demands on the set were outrageously selfish. Celebrities and the very rich are not the only people who become so egocentric, however. Egomaniacs can be people of all backgrounds and life circumstances.

- **The Judgmental and Sanctimonious** people of the world are also prime examples of ego out of control. Characterized by faces that "look down the nose," such people are convinced that they are the last word on everything. The penultimate fictional example of such a person is the character Miss Gulch, a.k.a. the Wicked Witch of the West, portrayed by Edith Hamilton in the classic movie *The Wizard of Oz*. For a more realistic example, the historic caste system in India causes people to define themselves in relationship to other castes, the "higher" looking down on the "lower."

The 7 Connections to Happiness and Harmony

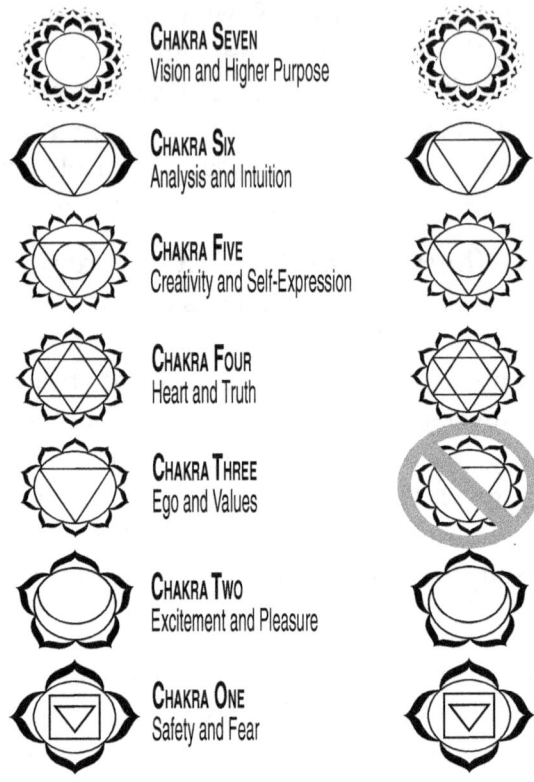

Third chakra blockages can limit access to higher chakras

Infinite Soul Veiled by our Ego

In my research into chakras and Eastern spirituality, I realized something special and wonderful. I was reminded that at the core, our souls are pure, good, virtuous, kind, harmonious, and loving. In other words, what our mothers have said is correct — "Doesn't matter what's on the outside, what matters is on the inside." The only thing that I would add is that at the core of all human beings, whether a saint or a criminal, is a soul quality of goodness.

Our third chakra is where our minds identify our selves as human beings. This means identifying ourselves in our professions, in our families, or in other ways. While we don't consciously realize it, the aim for most people is to feel good in

Chapter Three: The Chakra Three Connection – Ego and Values

some way about themselves. We will align ourselves with organizations and people that embody what we view as good. Some people who have excessive third chakras may derive enjoyment from hurting others. Why certain people act in a way that is hurtful goes in the opposite direction of the soul and is a secret for psychologists to uncover. Spiritually, we can say that such a person is still a pure soul who has lost his or her way.

Chakra Three Thought Patterns

Polarizing Viewpoints

Compared to chakra one and chakra two, chakra three is a more intellectual center. The focus of chakra three decision making is on defining ideas and information. Chakra three is not a chakra that is geared to complex or abstract thinking. Instead, chakra three is used to help us make concrete judgments.

The tendency for many operating at the chakra three level is judgment-oriented to extremes. Set-in-stone values and principles create confrontational face-offs with little chance, if any, that the opposing views will ever come to some kind of compromise. The mere mention of certain topics activates this polarization immediately. For example, observe how confrontational situations arise over such phrases as "right to life," "women's lib," stop the war," or "gun control." In the black-or-white mode of thinking, extenuating circumstances are not taken into consideration.

Many of us have worked with difficult people who have an attitude of "my way or the highway." We have also seen children demonstrate similar behavior by throwing tantrums. This extreme behavior comes from the point within us where we make a decision that ultimately is black or white. The third chakra is where ideas are converted into these black-and-white values and beliefs. In recent elections in America, this polarization has taken the form of visually labeling states as "red states" or "blue states," to indicate ballots cast for different parties. Such categorization insinuates a battle between opposing forces.

But we should remember that stimulation of the third chakra can be used as a positive force behind personal or national identity. Instead of being used to breed hate, it can be used to give the courage to win a war or fight for a just cause. Instead of stirring up

unreasonable anger, it can promote courage to strive for understanding between opposing forces. Used wisely, the third chakra is capable of producing statesmen instead of politicians, peacemakers instead of proponents of war.

Wedged into One Perspective

In addition to the overall ideology conflicts, which may happen on a larger political stage, these polarizing viewpoints can evolve into wedge issues that lead to conflict or disharmony. Wedge issues are those in which no other thought or idea is permissible because of strongly held biases. Such issues do not allow for any opposing thought, and anyone who attempts to present an opposing view is demonized. These perspectives are generally categorized as "hot topics," because they raise the fear that either something might be taken away from us (chakra one), that a personal gratification may no longer exist (chakra two), or that "my opinion" may not hold sway (chakra three). It is at this point that the ego becomes all important, to the point that the opinions of anyone who does not agree with my point of view is not allowed to speak. This can be a common challenge in marriage when both parties become wedged into immutable opinions without possibility of compromise. In the aftermath of senseless shootings in schools or malls, debate immediately springs up over gun control. Neither side is prepared to listen to the other. The advocates of gun control are focused on murdered students, while their opponents are focused on having their guns "pried from their cold, dead hands." Both sides of the question are wedged into an ideology that allows for no other possibility. What we see in these situations are issues like abortion, gay marriage, deportation of aliens, and the like, which continue to be debated without ever reaching any kind of resolution. The road sign might read: "Wedged Perspective Ahead, Mountaintop Thinking Must Not Pass."

Power Hunger

Another blockage to mountaintop thinking in the third chakra is an insatiable hunger for power. Dictators and despots are prime examples in the extreme of operating at the

CHAPTER THREE: THE CHAKRA THREE CONNECTION – EGO AND VALUES

third chakra level. Operating from the fear of not being in control (chakra one) and the possibility of not receiving personal sensory gratification (chakra two), the chakra three person is totally focused on personal power. He resists by whatever means available any attempt to reign in his grip on the power he craves. Thought ends right there, totally concentrated on the urgent need to maintain political power. It should not be construed, however, that level three thinking is limited to dictators and political tyrants. To some degree or other, this blockage occurs in much more everyday situations — the person who needs to be the president of the club, the bully on the playground, the domineering parent, or many others we might name. A disproportionate hunger for power becomes centered on the ego and limits thought to a focus on meeting the power goals.

Ego Reinforcement

Thought is locked in at chakra level three when reinforcement of the ego becomes the driving force in a person's life. This type of behavior is often seen in people who are constantly asking other people's opinions about something they have done. There is a story about an artist who painted a picture and asked a friend what he thought about the work. The friend said, "The subject matter is intriguing. Your use of color expresses the passion and emotion you wanted to present. Your technique is extraordinary, the way you use the brush strokes to highlight the movement with in the painting." When the friend finished his comments, the artist said, "I know. But do you really like it?" Examples like this might simply be artists who are insecure about their work, but they may also be the people operating from this chakra level who surround themselves with sycophants who constantly stroke their egos. As in the case of compulsive behaviors discussed in Chapter Two, such an egocentric focus is caught up in a loop from which there is no escape and has an endless need for gratification.

Vulnerability to Flattery

Ironically, while it may seem that the egocentric person is stronger and more independent, he or she is actually more vulnerable to outside influences. Egocentric people are pliable and easily influenced by others who give them the accolades they crave.

THE 7 CONNECTIONS TO HAPPINESS AND HARMONY

Such people may melt like butter with the right amount of flattery. Consider the employee who constantly flatters the ego of the boss. In that employee's mind, it is acceptable to use flattery and insincerity as a means to promotion or salary increase. To the other people in the business, who are usually aware of the behavior, it seems insincere and plastic. Often, the other employees are aware of such transparent manipulation while the boss is not — possibly because his or her ego is being stroked in ways that satisfy that his or her self image.

Values and the Third Chakra

The third chakra is also the chakra that allows us to connect with our values and beliefs. Over generations and generations, tribes, families, countries, and all mankind have developed values and beliefs based on past experiences. And through marriage and life lessons, we grow and progress in building our own combined set of values. While the source of our values and principles can be based on profound insight, religious scriptures, and family teaching, it can also be based on prejudices, fear, and very limited sets of information. In other words, we get ideas and process information from a variety of stimuli, from our fear chakra in Chapter One to our crown chakra that will be talked about in Chapter Seven. The third chakra is where the *rubber meets the road* and where ideas meet tangible actions, tangible beliefs. And once these values are formulated, they become our shortcuts for thinking.

Values from Upbringing

Children are trained early on in such values as the Golden Rule or morals they are taught from fables and stories, until

CHAPTER THREE: THE CHAKRA THREE CONNECTION – EGO AND VALUES

these values get etched in their minds. But children also tend to mimic their parents' ideologies without thought or reason, often formulating biases that remain with them throughout their lives. However, what that person defines as "right" may not be a universally accepted fact.

Gut Feelings and the Seven Chakras

In addition to making decisions based on conscious black-and-white definitions, there are certain adaptive behaviors which make their way into decisions. Gerd Gigerenzer, the director of the Center for Adaptive Behavior and Cognition at the Max Planck Institute for Human Development in Berlin, Germany, offers some unique perspectives on the topic of gut feelings. While his research does not directly touch upon chakras, his findings align with some of the thought processes and behavioral tendencies that are common in the third chakra and base chakra. He defines gut feelings as "a judgment that

(1) appears quickly in consciousness,

(2) whose underlying reasons we are not fully aware of, and is

(3) strong enough to act upon."

He goes on to say that "gut feelings result from simple rules of thumb which take into account evolved capacities of the human brain."[15] The rules of thumb that he references can help a person in more advanced mechanical functions, such as catching a baseball, as well as simplifying certain more cognitive decisions like selecting numbers for a lottery ticket.

According to Gigerenzer:

Logic and deliberate systems have monopolized the Western philosophy of the mind for too long. Yet logic is only one of the many useful tools the mind can acquire. The mind, in my view, can be seen as an adaptive toolbox with genetically, culturally and individually created and transmitted rules of thumb.[11]

As we relate his findings to the seven chakras, it is apparent that there are multiple chakras that work together as tools in decision making. The third chakra plays a unique role in helping us internalize certain lessons or rules of thumb for fast action.

At the most fundamental level, this relates to self-esteem — by being right, we feel good about ourselves. By supporting a moral cause, this helps us feel good about ourselves. Oftentimes, this means that we control our environment to allow inputs that reinforce our self-esteem. In political rallies, we rarely see events that integrate pro-life and pro-choice members. Unfortunately, we create an undue lopsidedness in our perspective when we constrain our inputs to just the ideas that we agree with.

Our Ego from the Mountaintop

Having a healthy ego is a motivator to make us productive; it gives us a moral compass and supports an overall definition of right, fairness, and goodness. It can seem like we are competing at odds with one another in times of war or disputing opposing ideologies and beliefs. Nevertheless, we should ultimately remember that beneath much of the disagreement are individuals who want to believe in the right cause and who want do to the right thing. It is possible to get so caught up in third chakra identity and ego that we lose track of the goodness that we want to harness. And it leads to many imbalances and, in many cases, highly inappropriate behaviors, which become blockages in our chakra system.

Making Important Decisions

What is needed for important decisions is an understanding and upholding of your own personal principles and values. The late Mother Teresa is an excellent example of doing for the community rather than for self-aggrandizement and business gain. On a smaller scale, but no less appropriate, business employees out in work clothes cleaning up a five-mile section of adopted highway are performing a public service for which they have no greater reward than the respect of the community at large.

The third chakra guides us in defining the world and our place in the world. Similar to chakra one and two, chakra three is a more instinctive, action-oriented chakra rather than a highly intellectual processing center. If we are not watchful, this chakra can move us toward decisions that reinforce our

CHAPTER THREE: THE CHAKRA THREE CONNECTION – EGO AND VALUES

self-esteem but lead us astray from our higher purpose or outcome. In decision making, a healthy third chakra, along with a balanced ego and a strong personal foundation of values, can guide us toward making our best choices. In the next chapter, we will see how everything begins to come together in the process of decision making, and no factor should be left out completely. Rather, we need to incorporate our awareness of all aspects of our natures into the formula for a fully awakened mountaintop perspective.

Secrets to Mountaintop Thinking

Mountaintop Thinking

▲▲ **SECRET #1:**
Detach Yourself Because It's Not About You

In Eastern thought, there is a heavy emphasis placed on detachment. There is a principle that suffering is a result of our attachments. When we lose money on an investment, we are unhappy because of our attachment to money. When we face troubles in the workforce and lose our job, we are unhappy because of the attachment we have to our jobs, the people, and the income. As we get older and start to see signs of aging, and the body we had when we were eighteen is no longer there, we are unhappy. While certain attachments are necessary for sustaining one's life and family, the extraneous attachments that we carry in our ego can become impediments to lasting happiness.

For example, oftentimes we utilize external symbols to define us as people — keeping up with Joneses. "I'll feel good when I drive a certain car, when I get accepted into Harvard, when I get that promotion." In other words, using the outside world to make us feel good about ourselves, when in fact, it should be the other way around; we should feel good about ourselves and reflect that inner confidence and happiness to the world. If we are not careful, with each stage of life, we continue to pile on more requirements on ourselves. If we are looking for outside forces to define us, we are in for a long, bumpy road. Because the only thing that is certain in our environment is uncertainty and change. This is pronounced today more than ever as companies undergo layoffs, nations experience food shortages, jobs are outsourced, homes are foreclosed, families are split up. If we latch on to these external aspects to define us,

The 7 Connections to Happiness and Harmony

then we are constantly attaching ourselves to things that are constantly changing. And we ultimately become the ping-pong ball that swings between two paddles in a match.

The irony of shedding our ego is that we can actually take more risks and think more clearly and increase our chances of success. Ego is like personal baggage. It's easier to backpack around Europe if packing lightly. If we don't have the heavy baggage of our ego keeping us tied to decisions based on the confines of status, self-identity, and polarizing dislike, we can focus on ideas, opportunities, and new solutions.

There is something beneficial materially and spiritually in setting goals and focusing on their successful completion. Therefore, the idea is not to become complacent or lazy. The idea is to maximize your ability to achieve anything you set your mind to by connecting more deeply with the goal rather than to the result of the goal.

▲▲ SECRET #2:
Become an Answer Seeker, Not a Definer

For those who have a very strong and active chakra three, there is a critical shift that should be made in the mindset. This is moving from a mindset of having all the answers and defining the world based on a set ideology to being someone who is continually seeking answers. Even when we are confident in the path we are taking and the beliefs we have, if we can adopt a mindset of seeking answers rather than having the answers, then we give ourselves access to more information. The third chakra moves from being closed to being open. The people who are the most receptive to information will ultimately be the ones who have the most information to make the best decision.

▲▲ SECRET #3:
Assume that Everyone Has Goodness Within Them

The tendency in chakra three is to demonize the opponent. As we look at chakra three and we consider things that we feel

CHAPTER THREE: THE CHAKRA THREE CONNECTION – EGO AND VALUES

passionate about, it's important to realize that behind every opinion is a person who is a kind, caring, good soul. If we start from the vantage point that each person has goodness, then our ability to accept people and listen to them and to incorporate their viewpoints into a larger picture improves.

▲▲ SECRET #4:
Don't Argue with a Chakra Three Person!

The term "butting heads" comes to mind when I think about chakra three. The aggression that people have gets manifested in our chakra three power center. And the result of that can be very harmful. When somebody has their mind made up and they get into aggression mode, they will not listen to you. So if the end goal is to reach a resolution of some sort, then maybe it's better to wait. Or it might be more effective to try alternative approaches or find other points in common. But by arguing with a chakra three person, there are no winners. The "perceived winner" will be the one who has the most intimidation and brut force.

▲▲ SECRET #5:
Create an Ego-Less Environment

I think that one of the most dangerous pitfalls in home life, in work life, and amongst nations is the ego. If we can make a dedicated effort to build environments that are focused on love, meaning, truth, and higher purposes (as we talk about in the upcoming chapters) versus environments which are focused on one-upmanship, excessive competition, anger, and conflict, we are allowing the creative and collaborative juices to flow through, rather than allowing thinking to be blocked at chakra three. I believe the answer to this is to align not with your status and personal ambition, but around the vision and higher values of your group. In his eulogy speech of the late Tim Russert, his son, Luke Russert, said the following words about his father: "Great men often lead with their egos. Tim Russert led with his heart, his compassion, and, most importantly, his honor. He had a great time living, and is no doubt having the time of his life now in heaven."

In Summary

- Chakra three is our self-identity or ego center. This chakra is the lens through which we look at ourselves and the world around us.

- Chakra three is also the center of hard work, will power, courage, and determination.

- Paying close attention to chakra three components results in avoiding the strictly black-and-white extremes in favor of well-rounded, more inclusive approaches.

- An overactive chakra three may lead us to serious decision pitfalls that overshadow the original objectives.

- A balanced ego can lead us to the best decisions.

CHAPTER FOUR

The Chakra Four Connection
The Heart Chakra

Just as New York's Grand Central Station provides a converging point for different trains, the fourth chakra is the converging point for thoughts and feelings across all the chakras. As our thought trains roll in from the base chakras with all of their emotional baggage, they meet up with intuition and higher thought patterns arriving from above. The heart chakra is the seat of our soul and a reservoir of memories, emotions, and truth. The heart chakra allows us to experience a multi-textured picture of the world around us.

We can visually track chakra four development in children as they become able to sense emotions other than their own. They begin to envision a wider world and larger patterns of behavior.

As these children mature into teenage and adult years, their capacity for love evolves and gets stowed away deep in the recesses of the heart chakra. In my own meditative experience, I have realized that the heart chakra is such a powerful connection that we create emotional walls or sheaths to hide our feelings from plain

sight. The top layer of our emotional sheath includes those raw visceral emotions, such as fear, excitement, anger, and lust, that can be traced back to the lower chakra feelings and sensations. However, underneath this sheath of raw feelings rests a deeper capacity of feeling that embodies compassion, empathy, friendship, and unconditional giving. The heart chakra allows us to connect with a larger and greater spiritual force of love.

Love is a topic that is discussed by many philosophers, songwriters, movie producers, and even political lawmakers. In most discussions, love is often spoken about in very finite and confined terms — whether that is between man and woman, parent and child, or just two friends. As we start to connect more deeply with our heart chakras, we realize that the capacity to love is limitless. Our love can grow to encompass a larger universe of people that extends far beyond the formal relationships and ties one has to others.

Defining the Heart Center

The fourth chakra is called *Anahata*, and in ancient Sanskrit, the word has the meaning of "unhurt, unstruck, unbeaten," referring to the idea of unstruck sound in the celestial realm.[16] The location of the fourth chakra is the region of the heart along the vertebral column, the cardiac plexus. It is in the very middle of the chakra system of seven and is related to love and truth. A healthy fourth chakra allows for loving deeply, feeling compassion, and attaining a deep sense of peace and centeredness. It is in this area wherein lies our inner sense of truth as in the expression, "I know in my heart."

A fourth chakra person is someone who leads a life that embodies truth and love. It is at this level that the tendency to do good resides, and the attributes of dedication and service become motivating forces. For the spiritual, this may include surrender to a guru or dedication to a cause.

CHAPTER FOUR: THE CHAKRA FOUR CONNECTION – THE HEART CHAKRA

Chakra Four

Location: Chest

Sanskrit Name: Anahata

Color: Green [17]

Attributes of the Fourth Chakra Person

The quintessential example of thought and action emanating from the heart center is Mother Teresa, whose concern for the destitute caused her to abandon what her brother, Lazar, described as being "well off" and "lacking nothing." Mother Teresa's efforts to help and educate the poor of India became legendary throughout the world and earned her a Nobel Prize.[18] Whether the love of a parent for a child or the selfless love of a Mother Teresa, this experience comes from the heart center of chakra four.

What We Feel in Our Hearts

Each of us has certain emotions that correspond with physiological sensations in our body. Most of these emotional sensations originate in the heart or chest area. For these senses,

THE 7 CONNECTIONS TO HAPPINESS AND HARMONY

we may use such terms or phrases as, "knowing in my heart," "gut instinct," "intuitive hunch," "women's intuition," or "my sixth sense." For the purposes of our discussion, I view all of these terms interchangeably as intangible forces. Chakra four is the collecting point from which all and any of these emotional sensations can be felt. Therefore, the question is not whether a certain sensation is a gut instinct versus an intuitive hunch, but rather, how to understand all the different sensations in order to build better decisions.

From the lower chakras, we receive the raw, base emotions such as fear, anxiety, and anger. Since these emotions can be overwhelming at times, at the point of making decisions it is best not to focus on those trains as they come in. Underneath all the emotions and feelings is a wellspring of knowledge ready to be tapped. From fear and angst to love and wisdom, the heart chakra is where it all comes together.

A fourth chakra person is one who rises above lower

Each Chakra is like an emotional layer or sheath felt in the heart Chakra

CHAPTER FOUR: THE CHAKRA FOUR CONNECTION – THE HEART CHAKRA

chakra impulses such as anger, lust, or jealousy. Instead, this person exerts influence on others through friendliness, kindness, patience, and calmness. The heart-centered person is someone who is considerate of others and wise. A fourth chakra person may be an outstanding parent, sibling, spouse, or child. That person becomes defined by a nature that includes friendliness and being loving toward others. Such a person unconditionally enjoys life — everything that is presented — without judgment — and will likely be considered "saintly" by others.

Examples of Fourth Chakra Behaviors

The most profound example of the opening up of the heart chakra occurs when an individual becomes a parent for the very first time. It is a special new capacity for love that extends far beyond one's normal comprehension of love, leading people to make great sacrifices to protect and nurture their children.

Friends offer a unique type of caring that is special in its own way because it is a voluntary contract between two people that is not tied to familial relationships, obligations, or responsibilities. Julia, who works in the office of one of my business associates, heard that her friend had lost his job and immediately called to see what she could do to help out the family.

And then there are special fourth chakra people such as Anna, an elderly lady who has survived all her relatives, who goes to a nursing home once a week just to visit with people who have otherwise been forgotten. "As long as I have the health to do this, I will," she said with a smile.

Operating from the Center of Emotions

The heart chakra is where our emotional center is. The heart chakra lies at the exact center of the chakra system; there are three base chakras below and three spiritual chakras above. Emotions are felt by most of us in our heart or chest area. Our feelings in the heart are not only powerful but, at times, overpowering, limiting our ability to see clearly and objectively, as in the case of blind love, guilt, or sadness.

Is Love Blind?

Love is such a powerful emotion that it can allow us to keep a blind eye to certain flaws. We can view those we care for with rose-colored glasses. (In the opposite case, we can also be extra harsh and have incredibly high standards for them!) While love can be blind, being blind to someone's flaws or problems provides an imbalanced perspective that may lead us down the wrong path in decision making.

I have been chided as being "blind" to the flaws of others. As a result, in order to look at people or situations honestly, a certain level of detachment must be exercised. This detachment involves looking at someone's actions not through rose-colored glasses, but with more objectivity. The objective analysis of actions allows us to understand the other person better. In that way, we can embrace the entire person with our hearts even though we may not agree with their actions.

Relationships and Loyalty

One of the most amazing characteristics of the human condition is our ability to build strong bonds of friendship and loyalty with others. Businesses, from the smallest mom-and-pop outlet to the largest multibillion-dollar corporation, are based, among other things, on key relationships. In the business world, I have seen the positive power of relationships in helping to ensure quality and trust. Yet I have also seen situations where loyalty may have prevented someone from taking a tougher stance in a hiring decision or in vendor selection. Relationships, while heavily dominated by the heart chakra, also help us to build a sense of comfort and inertia, which, in turn, stimulates our root chakra. In business, this is a type of switching cost. While it is always easier to stick with the status quo, one should not do so unwisely. A new mindset can be adopted which centers on building new bridges of friendship and loyalty.

Ridden with Guilt

Another powerful emotional force in our decision making is guilt. In our daily life, whether our work life or our home life, there are many situations that can trigger our inner guilt factory. I believe that guilt is a valuable emotion in allowing us to see the needs of others and to be considerate of those needs. Guilt can also be a tremendous motivator for taking action and setting priorities. However, the feeling of guilt is in itself very unproductive and can lead us down a path of unhappiness and reactive behavior.

There are times when we feel guilty because we are not fulfilling certain duties or obligations that are important. One example of this is in missing the death or passing of a loved one. While this may not always be possible, the best approach for handling guilt is to try to our best ability to get in front of guilt by proactively deciding one's priorities rather than allowing them to be decided by others. In other words, we should make decisions based on love instead of guilt. Just like fear, we should also learn to also say "no" to guilt.

Lower Chakra Emotions

The heart chakra is the converging point where we physically feel the pull of emotions from our root chakra all the way up to our seventh chakra. And given the power and pull of our emotions, the question we must ask ourselves is: How can we best use our heart chakra to guide us to making our best decisions? I guess the right answer is that we use the heart as a tool for uncovering the truth.

> *We hold these truths to be self-evident, that all men are created equal, that they are endowed by their Creator with certain unalienable Rights, that among these are Life, Liberty and the pursuit of Happiness.*
> — ***The Declaration of Independence***

The Inner Circle of Truth

Within each of us, we have something that I refer to as the inner circle of truth. This is like a magnet that allows us to attract ideas and information that ring true. Unlike the third chakra, the inner circle of truth is not about one's ego, personal agenda, or passing judgment. The inner circle of truth is about sensing whether something rings true. It's our own personalized truth detector.

THE 7 CONNECTIONS TO HAPPINESS AND HARMONY

> ### What Others Have Said:
>
> *Believe nothing just because a so-called wise person said it. Believe nothing just because a belief is generally held. Believe nothing just because it is said in ancient books. Believe nothing just because it is said to be of divine origin. Believe nothing just because someone else believes it. Believe only what you yourself test and judge to be true.*
>
> *[paraphrased]* — **The Buddha**

As we look deeply into the topic of truth, I believe that each chakra provides a dimension or unique puzzle piece into the overall truth. People will tend to see the truth from the chakra or level of consciousness that they commonly operate within. A person who operates from their fear chakra will look at the world differently than someone who operates from their heart chakra. The higher one progresses up the chakra stack, the greater their vantage point is into all of the different dimensions, and the more calibrated their inner sensor to detect the truths that are not easily detectable or observable. Discovering that "inner truth" involves an open, independent mind, free of personal biases and a willingness to expand. Against much conventional wisdom at the time, Christopher Columbus heard the voice within himself that told him the earth was round. His conviction was such that he influenced Queen Isabella and King Ferdinand of Spain to believe in him and finance his expedition. This historical example also illustrates how "inner truth" is mitigated as knowledge grows. Columbus's inner voice convinced him that he would be sailing off to India. It had not prepared him for the size of the planet or the idea that there might be whole continents that existed unknown to Europeans and Asians at the time.

CHAPTER FOUR: THE CHAKRA FOUR CONNECTION – THE HEART CHAKRA

That Which Does Not Ring True

Chakra four thinking will often result in the gut feeling that something "just isn't right." It raises the further question, "What's really going on here?" On a more personal level, this is easy to grasp. When a relative, spouse, or close friend suddenly behaves in a way that is not normal for that person, it is easy to sense that something is not right. Intrinsically, we understand when someone is unhappy or disturbed by something. It is a characteristic of the heart chakra to sense probable causes even when we do not have a great deal of information.

A key point to raise is that most people, while they have this inner circle of truth, oftentimes get so caught up in the noise that permeates their lower chakras — fear, excitement, groupthink, ego — that they don't take time to ask themselves (or ask their fourth chakra), "What do you think is really going on? Does this ring true?"

The Magnetism of Chakra Four

It is a pleasure when we can interact with people that operate from their fourth chakra. People who operate at the chakra four level often have many friends and tend to draw others to them. Most likely this is because chakra four people exude a positive calmness and pureness around which most others feel comfortable. Association with a chakra four person minimizes the fear of

---

What Others Have Said:

All truths are easy to understand
once they are discovered;
the point is to discover them.
— *Galileo Galilei*

I do not feel obliged to believe that the same God
who has endowed us with sense, reason,
and intellect has intended us to forgo their use.
— *Galileo Galilei*

judgmental reactions. Heart chakra people are the antithesis of those selfish, egocentric, and otherwise unpleasant individuals that people tend to avoid.

I recently talked with a man who met Nelson Mandela and the Dalai Lama while he was living in Bangkok, Thailand. It was not their celebrity, status, that had such a profound impact on him. His exact words to me about Mandela were, "If any man ever had cause to become bitter and combative, certainly this man did. But instead, I heard a man speak kindness and understanding from his very heart. He was unassuming and humble in his speech, talking informally to a room full of people who were hanging on his every word."

Interestingly, he used almost the same words to describe listening to the Dalai Lama, another man who has endured years of persecution without rancor or bitterness. These are the kind of people who, when they speak, you can hear the proverbial pin drop. These people who operate from the fourth chakra exude that kind of personal aura that, though unseen, draws people to them.

Some may say that these are people that follow the golden rule in being kind and compassionate to others. But it extends beyond the golden rule, because these are the people who demonstrate caring regardless of what is in store for them, how they are treated in return. They are not looking for equanimity, if they are operating in the fourth chakra. They are simply extending kindness because they want to be kind.

Eleanor Roosevelt was not noted for her beauty, nor for the quality of her voice, yet when she spoke, people listened because she had the fourth chakra characteristic of heartfelt thought.

As children develop further in their knowledge of themselves and their environment, they begin to take on fourth chakra characteristics. We have all heard of stories where children emptied their piggy banks to make donations to causes for children of the world who are less fortunate than they. Children are eager to send cards and well wishes to service men and women who are in foreign conflicts. American children have collected toys and games to send to Iraqi children. Such behavior is evidence of a developing fourth chakra. Unfortunately,

CHAPTER FOUR: THE CHAKRA FOUR CONNECTION – THE HEART CHAKRA

somewhere along the line, we lose sight of the compassion and caring that we had as a child. And sometimes it takes a more conscious effort to reconnect with our heart center.

> *The true measure of a man is how he treats someone who can do him absolutely no good.*
> — *Samuel Johnson (1709-1784)*

Physiological Reactions Associated with the Heart Chakra

Today, more and more research points to the relationship between thought and emotion in the psyche as people confront issues or make decisions. This is the fourth chakra component. When we operate from this level, actual physical sensations are frequently experienced as we confront situations that require benevolence, understanding, or special needs. These physical signals may occur even before we are consciously aware of what brings them on. Unexpected events may cause our eyes to widen and a feeling of tightness in the area around the heart. These are simply signals from the body. Anyone who has ever reacted tearfully to a feel-good movie has experienced this kind of heart-to-body connection.

It is not uncommon to hear people comment that something they heard or saw gave them goose bumps or made their hair stand up on end. Reactions such as these are directly connected to the heart chakra. Something seen or heard has struck a chord that resonates in the body, causing an observable physical reaction. The physiological connection between heart and body is an indicator of the emotional levels or layers that affect our thinking. From these experiences, we begin to elicit our individual truths.

> *There is a magnet in your heart that will attract true friends. That magnet is unselfishness, thinking of others first...*
> *When you learn to live for others, they will live for you.*
> — *Paramahasa Yogananda (1893–1952)*

THE 7 CONNECTIONS TO HAPPINESS AND HARMONY

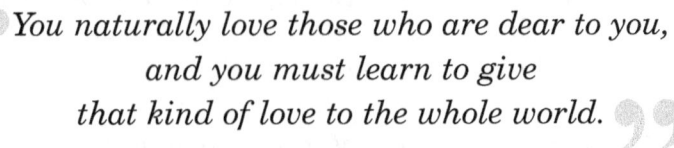

You naturally love those who are dear to you, and you must learn to give that kind of love to the whole world.
— **Paramahansa Yogananda (1893–1952)**

The question, then, is how to utilize the fourth chakra in our decision making. There are some obvious do's and don'ts in the process, as we consciously apply the chakra toward making business or any other kinds of decisions.

- **Do** listen to the heart when it is time to make choices. The heart can offer clues to wider networks of information that raw data cannot.

- **Don't** simply respond to what the heart says, as our lower chakra emotions and instincts can easily overpower objectivity and lead us in the wrong direction. It is building a relationship with the heart and learning to observe emotions rather than react to them.

- **Do** make sure that the important facts related to any decision resonate with your chord of truth. Listen to the heart when it insists on asking whether some plan of action actually "rings true."

- **Don't** become, as Albert Einstein once put it, a "slave to data." In doing so, we lock ourselves into a position of needing empirical proof to support any decision we make. The danger there is that data can be manipulated to provide the "proof" needed to make a decision. In contemporary times, there is probably no greater example of this fact than the lead-up to the Iraq war: To many people, the data simply did not resonate with either truth or prudence.

- **Do** look for authenticity in your relationships with others. Be aware that flattery is often not authentic

Chapter Four: The Chakra Four Connection – The Heart Chakra

and is dished out by those who want something in exchange. Look beyond any flattery to find open honesty, which may not always be what everyone wants to hear.

- **Don't** discourage honest input by others into the decision-making process. Doing so will effectively shut down vital information and contributions to the problem at hand.

- **Do** strive to make the best decision possible. Whatever we do in life has its effect on society as a whole, in addition to the repercussions for ourselves — either good or bad. This is true in our professional lives, within our families, and for our communities. We therefore owe it to ourselves as well as those around us to make the best decisions possible. In order to do that, we must develop a relationship with the heart. Such a relationship will remain open to new knowledge as it presents itself to us, which means that decisions made from the heart chakra are not carved in stone. They are, however, more reliable, because they are made from a combination of fact and intuition based on our life experiences.

By building the relationship with the heart, we take control of emotions rather than allowing emotions to control us. This model emphasizes the importance of the emotions coming from the base chakras, so long as we understand both *what* those emotions are and *where* they are coming from. The mountaintop thinking model is simple to comprehend:

- Collect the facts available
- Recognize the emotional responses within us
- Learn to understand "why" we have those emotions
- Assimilate the relevant data
- Admit gut hunches into the equation
- Put it all together and make a mountaintop decision

THE 7 CONNECTIONS TO HAPPINESS AND HARMONY

Secrets to Mountaintop Thinking

In chakras one through three, the aim has primarily been to find ways to balance and, in many cases, minimize the importance of these base chakras to focus more fully on the higher chakras. As we ascend to our discussion of the higher chakras, we are starting to think and activate the higher powers within us and the world around us. These higher powers are not always easy to articulate or comprehend through logic. However, these ideas begin to make more sense through personal experiences. The fourth chakra has a very special role in mountaintop thinking, as love is the glue which holds friendships, families, communities, countries, and the world together. In our lives, if we can create stronger attitudes and actions in favor of love and in service to others, this can greatly expand our individual happiness and lead us toward a path of greater material success.

▲▲ SECRET #1:
It's Not About You, It's About Those Around You

In our solo journey of life, we can oftentimes become too busy and too stressed to find time to even breathe, much less to think about the trials and tribulations of others. In our busy life, it is easy to lose sight of those around us, and it is easy to jump to quick judgments of others. In making certain decisions, I believe that making a concerted mental effort and shift to think about the needs of those around you will guide you in making better decisions. This not only allows you to think of a larger picture in making a decision, but also allows you to make a decision that has a bigger impact and that can ultimately solve a larger problem. This will also expand your reach and network of people who can offer their hands to assist you.

In the business world, there is an obligation to take care of stakeholders. In our own decisions, we should adopt that mindset and think about the shareholders in our life: the immediate shareholders and then those one or two steps beyond the immediate level. We ought to think about how our decisions impact those around us. In other words, make sure to bring compassion into your decision.

▲▲ SECRET #2:
Ignite Personal Passion

In making decisions and the appropriate trade-offs, it's important not only to think about the things that you are passionate about, but to make important choices and trade-offs which can be, if possible, in favor of igniting and awakening your personal passion. We will talk about this in more detail in Chapter Five, as personal passion is also linked to creativity. When we are working on projects that we enjoy, we get less tired because our energy is being supplied in part by the cosmic energy of the universe.

I have observed this in myself when I have very little interest to focus on such mundane tasks as doing laundry or washing dishes. However, when I have the opportunity to go shopping or pursue my own creative projects, I am able to tap an unending supply of energy. Not only does personal passion allow us to enjoy our time working, it is also a signal to us of the special talents we have that we can provide and contribute to the world.

▲▲ SECRET #3:
Share the Love

The human capacity to love and care for others is our most valuable attribute. Yet it is a tendency that is often suppressed. In today's society, there is a heavy emphasis on focusing on the needs of one's immediate circle at the expense of others outside of the circle. In mountaintop thinking, look for opportunities to dissolve these barricades and this arbitrary demarcation between one's inner circle and outer circle. Look for ways to create a larger circle of friends and look for ways to continue to expand this circle.

THE 7 CONNECTIONS TO HAPPINESS AND HARMONY

As we embrace others in our hearts, our capacity and understanding of love expands. Sharing our capacity and connection with others is actually simpler than we realize; at the core of humanity is the ability to love one another.

▲▲ SECRET #4:
Learn to Love Thy Adversary

At times we are fraught with situations in which we must work with an adversary to put together a winning proposal. In many cases, it can be very difficult to see eye to eye with someone whom you disagree with and dislike.

I believe that even in these situations, it is valuable to try to find a way to see the good in others. Fundamentally, underneath the veil of each of our personalities is a soul quality of kindness, honesty, and purity. If we can look for those soul qualities in the people we are working with, then we are better poised for creative problem solving in order to make our best possible decisions. While we may never condone the behavior of an adversary, we can always work to see the good that is more hidden.

▲▲ SECRET #5:
Employ an Expansive Approach to Dealings

In today's complex world, there are many difficult decisions and negotiations. In chakra three, we talked about the challenges that come with a polarizing perspective. Even in these challenging situations, the most successful people will be those who can find common ground. Look for ways to unite all the positive ideas together; look for ways to take the best of all worlds together.

In my conversations with South Asian leaders in my not-for-profit work, I have learned that many have faced serious challenges in balancing the cultural identity between East and West. The ones who appear to have the most comfort are those who have developed a mindset of taking the best from the cultures that they live in. They are, in effect, approaching their cultural identity with an additive mindset.

▲▲ SECRET #6:
Balance the Heart with the Head

In talking about chakra four, we can see that the heart chakra — human emotion — is both a powerful tool and something that can lead us astray to make fundamentally wrong decisions. Sometimes our emotions are so powerful that they can taint our perception and actions. We can end up making decisions that are both foolish and unwise. The best decisions are those where we strike a balance between the heart and head. We can make decisions that feel right in our heart and support the higher wisdom that is associated with our head (chakra six and seven).

In Summary

- Chakra four is our heart chakra. This chakra is the midpoint of all seven chakras.

- Chakra four is the seat of our soul where many of our past memories are stored.

- Chakra four is also the center of knowledge and truth.

- The heart chakra gives us capacity for love that extends beyond our immediate relationships to a larger universe of people.

- The capacity for love is so great that humans have developed emotional walls or sheaths to hide away their feelings deep in their heart chakra.

- Our best decisions are those that balance the truths felt in the heart with the rational logic and thinking in our heads (chakra six).

 **THE 7 CONNECTIONS TO HAPPINESS AND HARMONY**

CHAPTER FIVE

The Chakra Five Connection
Creativity and Self-Expression

One of the greatest eye-openers for me occurred when I learned that there was a distinct processing center in the system dedicated to *creativity* and *self-expression*. Up until this time, I had accepted the popular concept that there are some people who are the analytical type and others who are the creative type. Those were convenient pigeonholes for classifying people from surface observations. Yet there was always a part of me that felt uncomfortable about boxing people in according to those general criteria. It implied, to me, that creative people somehow lacked the ability to be analytical, while analytical people were devoid of any creativity. I realize now that my heart chakra was admonishing me to step back and take a closer look.

When I began to discover that there actually is a natural force in all people for creativity and self-expression, I developed a deeper understanding and appreciation of the capabilities of all humans.

A company that comes to mind as I consider the fifth chakra is the internet site and phenomenon known as MySpace.com. Created in 2003, the site is dedicated to allowing individual creativity and self-expression to anyone. MySpace has paved the way for an entire

The 7 Connections to Happiness and Harmony

industry of social networking websites and technologies.[19] People from all backgrounds and levels of education have jumped on the social networking bandwagon and the chance to express themselves and their creativity. The very success of MySpace testifies to the inner desire humans have for self-expression.

On MySpace, we see photographs, blogs, music, videos, and a number of artistic tools people can choose to let the world know who they are. These are people operating from the fifth chakra.

Chakra Five by Definition

The creativity and self-expression chakra is represented by the color blue and located in the area of the throat. Chakra five allows us to make our creative mark on the world. It is the chakra that allows us to express our thoughts and feelings. Chakra five enables us to express ourselves across the entire range of consciousness — from the gross physical level to our

Chakra Five

Location: Throat

Sanskrit Name: Vishuddha

Color: Light Blue [20]

CHAPTER FIVE: THE CHAKRA FIVE CONNECTION – CREATIVITY AND SELF-EXPRESSION

highest level of spiritual enlightenment. When we are thinking in accordance with our lower chakras (anger, excitement, fear, etc.), chakra five is the expression of our earthly desires and physical needs. When we are thinking with our higher chakras (heart, truth, analysis, intuition, wisdom), chakra five allows us to connect and share ideas that emanate from a larger spiritual force.

A chakra five person may be a creative writer whose self-expression takes the form of the written word. Singing, dancing, painting, sculpting, or any form of artistic expression belongs to this category.

Yet we should not limit our thinking of creativity simply to the arts. Einstein expressed himself both through his innovative mathematics and through eloquent expression of his thoughts. Creativity is very much a doorway for us to project our inner selves into the world as we seek to express ourselves publicly.

We add our own personal, creative touch to the work we do. The auto mechanic expresses himself through his expert workmanship. He takes obvious pride in working with his hands and his mind to accomplish his work. It is also a part of his creativity to find new ways to do the job. Out in the countryside, you may notice one farm that stands out because of the beauty and organization of its rows of crops, a fence line that is impeccably straight, and outbuildings that are well kept and painted. That farmer is expressing a great deal about himself though his farming. The possible ways to express oneself are as diverse and special as the number of individuals living on the earth.

What are the kinds of ways that you like to express yourself?

_____
_____
_____
_____

Expression in the Workforce

Perhaps the epitome of a successful enterprise with a decidedly chakra five bent would be Google. Management at Google encourages employees to spend twenty percent of their work time on projects that interest them. It is a radical innovation to encourage the creativity of chakra five throughout the company. The company is known for its relaxed working atmosphere and incorporation of humor into the workplace. Rather than be overwhelmed by the rapid advances in modern technological communication, Google has contributed even more possibilities.

Chakra Five
Business Implications

Word of mouth has always been an integral part of business. Through the advances of technology, the power of a consumer's voice has increased exponentially. Bloggers (yet another manifestation of today's platforms for communication and creativity) have vilified businesses whose products and services fail to meet reasonable standards. On one hand, there are individuals who write very thoughtful remarks and in-depth analysis of a particular topic. And on the other hand, many of the comments can be so offensive that the venue can feel like a virtual *Jerry Springer Show*, with strong words of hate, anger, and rage.

The Benefits of Human Creativity

Our creativity is our unique gift to the world. When we take time to communicate with others, share ideas, voice concerns, produce works of art, or create new equations or dance routines, all of these have a beneficial quality that affects people around us. Small contributions of creativity can produce a ripple effect that may be far-reaching beyond anything the originator could ever have imagined. A favorite recipe may find its way into millions of kitchens. An act of kindness tends to get passed on. In some instances, these contributions affect entire populations.

CHAPTER FIVE: THE CHAKRA FIVE CONNECTION – CREATIVITY AND SELF-EXPRESSION

Notable quotes about creativity

Curiosity is the key to creativity.
— **Akio Morita**

Above all, we are coming to understand that the arts incarnate the creativity of a free people. When the creative impulse cannot flourish, when it cannot freely select its methods and objects, when it is deprived of spontaneity, then society severs the root of art.
— **John Fitzgerald Kennedy**

All children are artists. The problem is how to remain an artist once he grows up.
— **Pablo Picasso**

The things we fear most in organizations — fluctuations, disturbances, imbalances — are the primary sources of creativity.
— **Margaret J. Wheatley**

The intuitive mind is a sacred gift and the rational mind is a faithful servant. We have created a society that honors the servant and has forgotten the gift.
— **Albert Einstein**

Odd how the creative power at once brings the whole universe together.
— **Virginia Woolf**

Creativity provides an often sorely needed sense of balance in life. For extroverts, the ability to express oneself verbally or visually is the all-important key to recharging one's personal batteries. Other people may be fulfilled by a close-knit circle of

relationships that offers a kind of intimacy important in self-expression. These close relationships provide a safe environment for venting pent-up emotions.

As children develop qualities of the fifth chakra, we begin to notice their artwork or other propensities for self-expression. Even with their limited knowledge and experience, children at this stage will experiment with other ways of tackling a problematic situation when their first attempt fails. Their creativity is fuelled by their curiosity and often manifests in amusing or astonishing ways.

Reading the many quotes from notable thinkers of the world sheds important light on the necessity for creativity in our lives, our thinking, and our decision-making processes. It also emphasizes the idea that creativity need not be a *Mona Lisa* or "Ode to Joy." Creativity may equate for some people to a way of life, like the medical research scientist looking for the cure of disease or the engineer designing the next gadget. We have observed this kind of creativity in people like Bill Gates and Steve Jobs. On a less grand scale but equally creative are those people who find their fulfillment in performing their jobs well.

All creativity, from whatever level, has universal benefits. From the comedian who makes people laugh to the rocket scientist who helps put a man on the moon, creative people benefit society.

The Spiritual Current of Creativity

The act of being creative or working on a creative project offers each of us an opportunity to connect with a higher spiritual experience. Whether an Olympic athlete, a pianist, or even a gifted orator, there is a flow of spiritually charged energy that allows ordinary people to accomplish extraordinary achievements. Each of us, as a human, is endowed with special creative talents or areas that we are naturally attuned to. As we cultivate these gifts, we are actually connecting with something larger and more uplifting than we realize.

CHAPTER FIVE: THE CHAKRA FIVE CONNECTION – CREATIVITY AND SELF-EXPRESSION

Blockages to Chakra Five

From a seven chakra perspective, we can lead a life that is more fulfilling and rewarding as we start to focus on our energies and capabilities hidden away in our higher chakras. The lower chakras (chakras one–three) are so powerful that they tend to overpower the use of the higher chakras in daily decisions. The overuse of one or more of the lower chakras is called a blockage. The question still remains: Is there such as a thing as a higher chakra blockage?

The answer is, "Absolutely." If we focus on our higher chakras and neglect the importance and practical needs of our lower chakras, then we are neglecting our duties in the world.

In Jeannette Walls's captivating memoir *The Glass Castle*,[21] she talks about her childhood experiences set against the backdrop of decrepit conditions. While Walls never relates her experiences to the seven chakras or yoga principles, her memoir depicts a startling example of a chakra five blockage that led to overall irresponsible, neglectful conditions. Wall's brilliant, charismatic father and artist mother focused on their pursuits of creativity and excitement, leaving their children to fend for themselves regarding food and other basic necessities. While Walls and her siblings were starving for food, her mother was pursuing an unrealistic path of becoming a painter, while her father was unable to hold down a job due to alcoholism. The Walls family was forced to move from city to city to avoid creditors and at times go without food. While it's evident that in this case, her parents derived great enjoyment from their higher chakras, their enjoyment was at the expense of fulfilling their duties as parents to provide a safe, stable environment for their family.

The creative pleasure that is stimulated in the fifth chakra has a ripple effect to the chakra two pleasure center. The intensity of chakra five (and other higher chakra experiences) can be so electrifying that dangerous combinations of narcissism, addictions, or plain laziness that may result. In the case of the mother in *The Glass Castle*, she was a self-proclaimed "excitement addict" who not only indulged her passion for painting, but also her excitement for

The 7 Connections to Happiness and Harmony

moving and facing dangerous situations. This prevented her from keeping a job and providing adequate shelter and food for the family. The higher chakras can provide such fulfillment and enjoyment for some that it may be tempting to forget about duties and responsibilities. However, one's enjoyment of higher chakras should not cause suffering to others. Duties and responsibilities should not be neglected for creative enjoyment.

A different yet related type of blockage occurs with individuals who are "all talk and no action" or "great idea people." These are individuals who enjoy the creative aspects but ultimately do not turn the creative thoughts into tangible action. Hence, they may be heavily focused on the fifth chakra but are not able to connect those thoughts to the lower chakras for action.

Creativity Without Boundaries

There is an old popular song that says, "Don't fence me in." Not all fences around creativity, however, come from external sources. It is possible to over-think some creative impulse to the point where action is impaired. You may know someone who has talked about some great business idea for the past twenty years without ever making an effort to initiate the project.

Part of being free and without boundaries is to be as open and receptive as possible, allowing natural creativity and self-expression to come out. I vividly remember learning this in my violin practice as I carefully, consciously tried to keep track of my fingers and control their movement. I never seemed to be able to keep up; but when I let myself become immersed in the music, the experience became truly enjoyable. Instead of trying to control the sound and movement, I tapped into a creative universe of sound that became a product of my expression. The music also sounded better when it came from the heart, because heartfelt music expresses what we know and feel. A friend of mine who is an accomplished violinist once told me about her teacher, who said that "in order to play well, one needs to experience life." Since she was very young at the time, the teacher gave her a very sad book to read. After reading this story the young artist began the process of awakening and expressing her inner emotions.

Myths About Creativity – Especially in Business

A great deal is said about creativity in the workplace these days, yet little is actually known about where breakthrough ideas come from. A mythology has grown up to suggest motivation for creativity; but it appears to be just that — mythology. Researcher Teresa Amabile, who heads the Entrepreneurial Management Unit at Harvard Business School, has worked on discovering the sources of creativity in business for some thirty years, and she has debunked many commonly held beliefs about creativity.

- ### *MYTH #1:*
  Creativity Comes from Creative Types –

  Not so, says Professor Amabile. "There's this common perception among managers that some people are creative, and most aren't. That's just not true. As a leader, you don't want to ghettoize creativity; you want everyone in your organization producing novel and useful ideas…"

- ### *MYTH #2:*
  Money Is a Creativity Motivator –

  A misconception, according to Professor Amabile. "Our research shows that people put far more value on a work environment where creativity is supported, valued, and recognized."

- ### *MYTH #3:*
  Time Pressure Fuels Creativity –

  Again, not so according to the research. "Time pressure stifles creativity because people can't deeply engage with the problem. Creativity requires an incubation period; people need time to soak in a problem and let the ideas bubble up."

- **_MYTH #4:_**

    Fear Forces Breakthroughs –

    Think again. "The entries show that people are happiest when they come up with a creative idea, but they're more likely to have a breakthrough if they were happy the day before."

- **_MYTH #5:_**

    Competition Beats Collaboration –

    "In our surveys, we found that creativity takes a hit when people in a work group compete instead of collaborate. The most creative teams are those that have the confidence to share and debate ideas. But when people compete for recognition, they stop sharing information."

- **_MYTH #6:_**

    A Streamlined Organization Is a Creative Organization –

    After studying a large company downsizing over an eighteen-month time frame, the evidence belied this assumption. "Anticipation of the downsizing was even worse than the downsizing itself — people's fear of the unknown led them to basically disengage from the work. More troubling was the fact that even five months after the downsizing, creativity was still down significantly." [22]

From Dr. Amabile's studies, it is clear that high stress factors suppress creativity. Furthermore, the study supports my eye-opening realization that creativity is not limited to the creative types but is present in everyone. As in the seven chakras, this study takes a much more expansive view of creativity that includes everyone.

CHAPTER FIVE: THE CHAKRA FIVE CONNECTION – CREATIVITY AND SELF-EXPRESSION

Copyright 2001 by Randy Glasbergen.
www.glasbergen.com

"My team is having trouble thinking outside the box. We can't agree on the size of the box, what materials the box should be constructed from, a reasonable budget for the box, or our first choice of box vendors."

Secrets to Creative Thinking from the Mountaintop

▲▲ **<u>SECRET #1</u>:**
Create an Environment
that Is Receptive to Expression

When we are at the height of creativity, we are tapping a larger pool or working with a larger spiritual force to guide us to find an innovative answer or solution. In other words, we want to create an environment both physically and emotionally that allows for creative ideas to rise to the surface. That includes creating an environment that is positive and safe for communication. This environment should be devoid of lower chakra baggage of fear, excessive excitement, or ego.

In the family environment, this means creating an atmosphere where the family communicates frequently and openly. And an environment where the children can share issues and challenges with their parents without fear of being punished or disciplined.

This same environment of free-flowing sharing of information

works effectively in the work setting as well. For example, during the brainstorming process, the official technique most often used is one where people contribute ideas before any critique of the ideas happens. This encourages the flow of ideas by soliciting a number of ideas and keeping the creative juices flowing by keeping egos out of the creative process. Each idea contributed receives equal attention and consideration before any consensus is drawn.

> **How receptive is your home or work environment to creative thinking?**
>
> _____
> _____
> _____
> _____
> _____

▲▲ SECRET #2:
Define a Time, Place, or Process for Creative Thinking

The ideal work environment is one that is safe and stimulates creativity. Unfortunately, in today's challenging economic times, the work environments are often warrens for stress. The stressful work environment hampers the natural creativity of teams. Similarly, stress at work influences our stress at home. Our personal lives are oftentimes even busier as we try to balance all our responsibilities. However, if we do not take time out to think about our professional or personal goals, we miss many opportunities for greater success. Therefore, as life becomes more stressful, it is even more important to schedule time for creative thinking.

Creative ideas and inspiration come to people in different ways. For some, they come in the middle of a conversation. For others, ideas come while washing dishes or walking their dog. For others, it is while writing a blog. There is no one

Chapter Five: The Chakra Five Connection – Creativity and Self-Expression

formula for creativity that works in all cases. However, for each person it's valuable to set aside some time for creative thinking, preferably when there is as little stress as possible.

Many companies choose off-sites for brainstorming meetings to create a neutral atmosphere uncluttered by the reminders constantly present in the corporate office. Such planning can be productive; however, if after the meetings employees return to high-stress situations, there is no support for a culture of creativity. The entire atmosphere of the business needs to resonate with the vibrations of creativity. It is precisely the Google kind of business model that stimulates growth and development. Metaphorically, the right atmosphere allows the fifth chakra to breathe.

▲▲ **SECRET # 3:**
Listen for the Vibration

Just as Chakra four has various levels of truth that correspond to the lower to higher chakras, the tone and vibration quality of our voice can shed some insight into the chakras that are being dominated in a particular decision topic. For example, when we are scared, our voices will show a level of fear and stress. When we are excited, angered, happy, our voices will reflect those different energies. As we pay closer attention to our own speaking and the style of communication of others around us, we can start to develop a deeper understanding of the energies and emotion surrounding a discussion.

Don't Be Stingy with Ideas – Share the Wealth of a Good Idea

For those who are heavily tapped into their fifth chakra, they will agree that there is never a lack of ideas. In many cases, these individuals will express a continuous flow of good ideas. Unfortunately, there is never enough time or resources to focus on all the ideas that are expressed. As good as an idea is, it has limited market value until it is implemented. I have seen many entrepreneurs that have clung to their ideas with secrecy, unwilling to disclose them to others. Unfortunately, what this does is limit their exposure to feedback and other possible creative discussions and ideas that can piggyback off of the original idea.

Unfulfilled Potential

In the journey of life, we are ultimately limited by the ideas we have. For example, if a student from the inner city decides to join a gang instead of attending college, it is unlikely that he can ever consider a career in medicine or law. If a couple decides to not save for retirement, they may ultimately fall short in their savings, as they get closer to retirement.

There is a natural skepticism that most people have when making plans, creating a vision, or imagining the future. While it's natural to feel skeptical, we should realize that it is impossible to touch the stars if we don't decide to reach for them. Each idea and smart action allows us to move closer to our ultimate goal or vision. Therefore, it's important to keep dreaming and to be as creative as possible. The environment that we surround ourselves with also plays a key role in helping to shape our ideas and aspirations. The more exposure we develop, whether that is to different professions, people, countries, or culture, the more our world opens to new ideas and possibilities that we had not imagined or envisioned before.

Notable Quotes About Imagination

The opportunities of man are limited only by his imagination. But so few have imagination that there are ten thousand fiddlers to one composer.
— **Charles F. Kettering**

The problems of the world cannot possibly be solved by skeptics or cynics whose horizons are limited by the obvious realities.
— **John F. Kennedy**

CHAPTER FIVE: THE CHAKRA FIVE CONNECTION – CREATIVITY AND SELF-EXPRESSION

Connecting the Dots

By this time, as we look at the usefulness of understanding the chakras and how that knowledge produces mountaintop thinking, we begin to see more clearly how these various levels all work together. It is impossible to discuss the higher chakras without reference to the base chakras as either motivating factors or potential blockages.

Gradually we are coming to see how all the chakras work in tandem to allow for that clear thinking which enables us to connect the dots of interrelated information. In the big picture of mountaintop thinking, the creativity and communication of chakra five play a pivotal part. Chakra five provides the inspiration and intuition necessary to assimilate and evaluate the information at our disposal as we set about making business, political, and personal decisions with clarity and conviction.

In Summary

- The fifth chakra is the creativity and self-expression chakra located in the throat area.
- This chakra relates to self-expression in all respects, from speaking to artistic expression to our personal contributions to the world.
- All humans have certain natural creative tendencies.
- Life is more fulfilling when we cultivate our fifth chakra and explore our own personal creativity.
- Through creative thinking, we set ourselves up for aiming higher in our goals.
- Creative thinking happens as a result of creating an environment that has less stress from the lower chakras.

THE 7 CONNECTIONS TO HAPPINESS AND HARMONY

Chapter Six

The Chakra Six Connection
Analysis and Intuition

The sixth chakra is considered the home of rational analysis and thinking. Sometimes called the "third eye," an awakened chakra six sees beyond the obvious. At this level, we are talking about a loftier level of thinking that is objective and detached from personal bias and emotion. It involves the analysis of collected data and stimulates our core intuition.

The term *intuition* is used broadly in our vocabulary to refer to any thought or feeling we have that we cannot directly put our finger on or explain. In effect, we have seven chakras which offer us seven levels of intuitive perception. Each of these seven chakras allows us to perceive a certain class or category of information. However, for our purposes, I refer to *intuition* solely in the context of sixth chakra intuition or through the third eye. Sixth chakra intuition comes to us in a spiritually guided fashion. The sixth chakra operates like a radio that receives signals from the universe. Just as an idea will come to us, intuitive perceptions radio in to us through our third eye. Third eye insights occur when we are calm, open, and receptive. The insights themselves are powerful and clear while also nonjudgmental.

THE 7 CONNECTIONS TO HAPPINESS AND HARMONY

In contrast to the sensations and hunches felt in the heart, third eye intuitions can feel less personal, as these intuitions come from the "head" rather than being felt in the "heart."

Chakra Six

Location:
Middle of Forehead

Sanskrit Name:
Ajna

Color: Indigo [23]

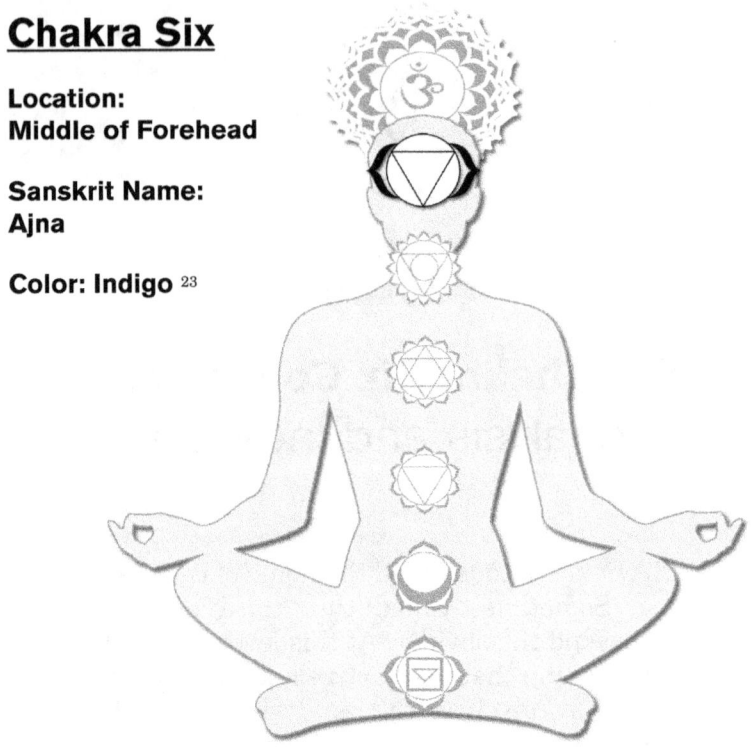

> *The rational mind (from ratio, "to count") thinks in pieces. One piece follows another, leading us logically from one thought to the next. While the rational mind may synthesize a whole from its individual pieces, it is poorly suited for grasping larger wholes on an immediate, experiential level. To grasp concepts of cosmic and transcendent consciousness — the realms associated with the upper chakras — we must have a more direct means of perception. This is the purpose of intuition.*
> — *Anodea Judith* [24]

Chapter Six: The Chakra Six Connection – Analysis and Intuition

However, some intuitive insights from our third eye resonate so deeply with us that they cause sensations or feelings in the heart, chest, or other areas of the body based on our memories, experiences, or personal needs.

Just as in Chapter Five, we saw that creativity is a faculty that all humans possess, here we discover that intuitive perception is a faculty that all humans have. Eastern Yogis will teach that as immortal souls, we come into this life with tendencies and talents from past lives. Someone who is a great artist may have been an artist sometime before. Therefore, our soul evolves with each life.

The aim of Yoga principles is to evolve our souls to someday reach a stage of enlightenment, realization, nirvana, or special form of astral heaven. In order to evolve spiritually, one must continue to evolve intellectually so that one's mind can be flexible and capable of experiencing and understanding the greater force of the universe. The continuance of learning and the focused effort on building one's intuitive faculties is very important for that goal.

In simple terms, rational thinking, knowledge, and education give us a foundation. Yet this is just the starting point. Knowledge and facts are not as important as the direct insights, ideas, and patterns that you see in the data, ultimately allowing you to cut through the clutter. In my perspective, there are phases or categories of understanding chakra six.

The Three Elements of Chakra Six

The Foundation of Chakra Six: Rational Thinking

Rational thought, as defined by the educational system, is the ability to put concrete pieces of information together to come up with a concrete answer, e.g., one plus one always equals two. In other words, the rational can only be expressed in some quotient of integers. Educational systems focus mainly on the rational thinking

The 7 Connections to Happiness and Harmony

"In the corporate world they pay you big bucks for thinking outside of the box!"

skills of students. Sometimes we forget that rational thinking is just the foundation and not the endgame. Rational thinking is just a starting point and foundation for building a mind that is efficient and flexible for use in deeper discoveries.

The Second Element: Pattern Recognition

The facts and knowledge we gain help us uncover new solutions, new ideas, or answers to problems. The thought processes and the relevant connections we make offer a demonstration of the sixth chakra at work and of mountaintop thinking. By applying knowledge to new challenges, we are applying our mental abilities in a positive and adventurous way. As an example, let us look at a twelve-year-old girl standing in a spelling bee. She has just been given the word *pharmaceutical* to spell. As she scans her database of knowledge, she may make several connections that have nothing to do with the letters necessary to spell the word correctly. She may almost subconsciously associate the word with Greek, where a *ph* takes the *f* sound. She may think of syllables that rhyme or are the same as in the word

Chapter Six: The Chakra Six Connection — Analysis and Intuition

nautical. Intuitively, she discards the irrelevant such as the *au* in *nautical* before she comes up with the correct spelling.

This illustration is not a profound example of quantitative analysis, but it does illustrate the sixth chakra assimilation of patterns that assist in coming up with the correct answer. Malcolm Gladwell discusses this very notion of pattern recognition in his book *Blink*, referring to what he calls thin-slicing. He defines thin-slicing as the ability of our unconscious minds to find patterns in situations and behavior based on very narrow slices of experience. Finding patterns in data and information, is an important processing activity of the sixth chakra.

The Third Element: Third Eye Intuition

Finally, the third element of our sixth chakra is also our third eye — our ability to directly perceive ideas and information. Sri Aurobindo, Indian nationalist, scholar, poet, mystic, evolutionary philosopher, Yogi, and guru, has described intuition as "the flash of a match in the darkness. For one brief moment, the whole room comes to the light. We can see its size and shape and the furniture and objects within it as an immediate whole experience. The flash of intuition is a momentary illumination of the psyche that reveals its underlying wholeness. As we grow in awareness (especially through meditation practices), we learn to sustain these illuminated moments for longer and longer periods." [25]

Most people have a certain level of undeveloped intuition that is felt as a hunch, or felt in moments of clarity or insight. With time and dedication, individuals can start to develop their own third eye intuitive faculties through the practice of mediation.

Communication Challenges with Intuition

In today's modern society, emphasis is placed on the use of rational tools and methods for uncovering solutions. Rational methods are important and necessary for providing all people with a structured set of principles that is relatively untainted by emotional biases. However, while it is important to apply rational

THE 7 CONNECTIONS TO HAPPINESS AND HARMONY

methods for analysis, it is also important that we start to develop our intuitive faculties to guide us in accessing a wider assortment of information. Our intuition can help us find new ideas and solutions or sense trouble before it happens. Therefore, while we want to be disciplined in understanding and applying rational tools and approaches, we should not allow ourselves to become slaves to data. Rather, the greatest thinkers and scientists are those who remain mentally flexible and receptive to new, intuitive insights.

Sometimes, our intuitive flashes can feel like a text message delivered directly to our foreheads! Other times, information can flow in like a fountain. Intuitive insights can be challenging to express, convey, or prove through rational data. As a result, many rational-oriented people often repress their intuitive faculties and choose to not listen to their inner voice. Christopher Columbus intuitively felt that the world was round and stood up to many skeptics who disbelieved his theory.

Fortunately for us, Christopher Columbus did not back down on his intuitive hunch, and we should not discard our intuitive hunches. Our hunches might be difficult to articulate or immediately measure. And as a consequence, we may face some opposition, laughter, or scrutiny from others. However, just because something is not easy to articulate or prove does not make it any less true. Our intuition gives us insight into a realm of information that is by design not directly accessible through facts and rational approaches. Our intuition can help us detect a problem before it festers into something greater. So while something may feel like a vague hunch, it is better to evaluate it than to discard it. Ultimately, if our intuitive hunch is correct, it will stand up to the rigor of the right testing.

School Day Recollections

As I reflect on my school days, I recall feeling awed by my classmates who appeared to be exceptionally brilliant. I would ask myself how in the world they could come up with the correct answers so quickly. Then I would think about the geniuses of the world, like Mozart, Beethoven, Thomas

CHAPTER SIX: THE CHAKRA SIX CONNECTION – ANALYSIS AND INTUITION

Jefferson, Robert Oppenheimer, and Albert Einstein, and wonder if they somehow inherited a special "genius gene" that set them apart from the rest of the world. I now realize that a true genius is one who can tap into the universe for ideas and inspiration — like holding a season pass to an amusement park so that they can come and go as they please.

The truth is that everyone is born with the capacity to tap the universe for insight. Many people, however, never become aware of that ability within themselves and, therefore, never take the time and effort to nurture it. The complication here is that we live in a culture today that still values the logic based on hard data over intuition. We are skeptical of feelings and hesitant to follow our hunches. In the old *Star Trek* TV series, it was tacitly assumed that the purely analytical Mr. Spock was the most brilliant man on the ship. Nevertheless, the intuitive thinking of Captain James Kirk always proved to be right when crucial decisions needed to be made. Mr. Spock may have scored off the charts on a standard IQ test, but Captain Kirk was aligned with a different set of frequencies in the universe.

It was, in fact, this very process of a chakra six flicker of intuition that awakened my interest in the seven chakras as a path for decision making. As I read about the chakras, something resonated deeply. That sensation caused me to begin reading voraciously all that I could find of the literature relating to the

---

**Albert Einstein,
both genius and spiritual thinker, observations:**

- Imagination is more important than knowledge.

- We can't solve problems by using the same kind of thinking we used when we created them.

From a sign hanging on his wall at Princeton University:

- Not everything that counts can be counted, and not everything that can be counted counts.

chakras. Day by day, new insights emerged for me in those flashes of recognition as the pattern began to take shape.

Arriving at Mountaintop Chakra Six Thinking

Our thinking does not need to produce anything as mathematical as the theory of relativity for it to be operating from the sixth chakra. When we suddenly see clearly the answer to any perplexing problem when simple rational solutions have failed to satisfy, we are operating at the sixth chakra level. The intuition of the sixth chakra is not emotional, intangible, or false; quite the opposite, it is a highly defined flicker of intellect. This kind of thinking can be applied to life situations, business solutions, or important decisions with which we are faced. The answers may come in one great flash of insight or in a series of flickers that guide our actions.

At this stage in our thinking, the ability to make the connections that result in clear understanding comes to the surface. It is also the point at which we can weed out irrelevancies, which are also a kind of blockage. Thinking at this level, our syllogisms will ring true because we are observing from the mountaintop.

Nearing the Pinnacle

When we learn to think and make decisions from our chakra six abilities, we have come near the mountaintop. What we have up to this point is a model for higher thinking that will guide us in making informed decisions. It will help us understand group dynamics and how to deal with different personality types. We will be able to see with our mind's eye what is invisible to our optical organs. We now have the ability to collect more information and are prepared to sift through it and apply what is relevant and important. We can cast better votes, make better choices, and enjoy a better quality of life.

CHAPTER SIX: THE CHAKRA SIX CONNECTION – ANALYSIS AND INTUITION

Secrets to Mountaintop Thinking

Mountaintop Thinking

▲▲ **SECRET #1:**
Cultivate a Stronger Mind

As talked about earlier in this chapter, the notion of intelligence tends to be one that is viewed in very finite, definitive terms. The idea is that we are born with a set aptitude or level of intelligence that we use within the boundaries of in our careers and in all facets of living. The notion is also that as we get older, our memory and other faculties weaken. From a spiritual perspective, this is actually a misnomer. I believe that as humans, we have the potential to get smarter with age. Certain faculties, such as our memory, may diminish with age, but our intuitive intelligence grows and expands with effort. Our intuitive intelligence is not tied to the age of our body, but to the connection our soul has with the larger universe. As we establish and build this connection, our access to information and our overall understanding of worldly matters goes up.

However, just as an Olympic athlete must actively exercise and stretch in order to prepare for the tournament, intuition is a faculty that must be cultivated with effort and attention. Building intuitive skills begins with keeping our analysis skills in tip-top shape through continuous learning. Also, as you look at your overall activities, try to shift some of them from passive activities like watching television and movies to activities that engage your mind in learning. As our Olympic athlete needs to continually be

> **What kind of activities do you engage in to keep your mind healthy?**
>
> _____
> _____
> _____
> _____

training, we should be keeping our minds in similar shape. Also, the more knowledge we gain, the more we are able to understand the world around us.

As I hear and read about various enlightened saints, there is one common message that comes through. In order to be able to receive the spiritual wisdom of the universe, the mind must be open and receptive enough to receive that information. Hence, making an effort to keep furthering one's intellectual understanding will help in future spiritual pursuits.

▲▲ SECRET #2:
Develop a Can-Do Mindset with Tough Subjects

Most people had a particular subject in school that was not their strong suit. For many, it was math, while for others, it might have been reading or science. Unfortunately, this weakness we have, if left unchecked, can actually turn into a mental block that prevents us from applying that knowledge when we need it. As we talk about the analytical dimension of the sixth chakra, there is a level of adventure we should develop to explore new subjects and subjects for which we may feel weak, or less in our safety zone. Whether we jump with both feet into a new subject or take baby steps, the key is to develop a mindset of being adventurous and open to data, information, and new subjects. Each subject we study gives us a larger base of knowledge from which to draw in finding new ideas and solutions. More importantly, this mindset of adventure helps us build confidence, which is ultimately needed in mountaintop thinking.

In highly competitive environments, it is easy to lose confidence and to lose hope. However, at the end of the day, the learning process is spiritually guided. Beyond the professors, beyond the textbooks, beyond the classrooms, beyond the grades, is the discovery of knowledge. The process can be both valuable and gratifying.

CHAPTER SIX: THE CHAKRA SIX CONNECTION – ANALYSIS AND INTUITION

> **Are there certain subjects you like to avoid?**
> **Have you considered embracing these subjects?**
> _____
> _____
> _____
> _____
> _____

▲▲ SECRET #3:
Use Data as a Window into a Larger Truth

There is a tendency to confuse data and knowledge with the guiding principles and truths that they support. As we evaluate data, we should look at data as a window into a larger story. Rather than looking at data as the final summation of knowledge, we should think of it as a starting point for digging into deeper causes and meanings. We should not consider the data as *being* the truth, but as a tool for digging into the truth. In other words, we would be *empowered* rather than being *overpowered* by the data. A truly sixth chakra leader, therefore, uses data as a tool for understanding a larger truth rather than becoming a slave to data as the definition of truth.

▲▲ SECRET #4:
Meditate or Find Activities Like Yoga
that Lend Themselves to Inner Calmness

In decision making, a calm, clear mind is always better than a frazzled, frantic mind. Unfortunately, in our busy lives, it can feel like we are running a mile a minute with very little time for thinking. Our anxieties can be so high that it is difficult to feel calm. But the irony is that when our anxieties are at their highest, we need to make the strongest effort to find inner calmness. Each of us has different techniques that work for relaxing, whether

THE 7 CONNECTIONS TO HAPPINESS AND HARMONY

having a healthy diversion such as spending time with family and friends, or listening to music. Hatha Yoga helps us connect with our inner spirit and therefore helps us develop a deeper calmness. Pantanjali, one of the ancient seers and originator of the Yoga Sutras, felt that the physical postures of Yoga were important for preparing the body for deep mediation. Meditation is a valuable path for developing inner calmness. As we talked about in Chapter Five regarding creativity, it is valuable to set aside time for calm inner reflection.

Previously, I had many misconceptions about meditation. I felt that meditation was difficult and an activity of intense focus that only a few people could do. I did not feel that I had the inner concentration to control the mind. And early on in my practice, I was applying so much focused pressure on my forehead that I started getting headaches! After quite a few of these headaches, I sought out some assistance and guidance with my meditation. After seeking help and after meditating in a group setting with others, I learned that my approach to meditation was all wrong! The whole idea of meditation is not to tense up and focus the mind on one idea but simply to mentally relax and to enjoy being relaxed. And when I learned that I could find tranquility with my meditations, I found them very relaxing, and I have noticed a remarkable change in my calmness.

Thought for Quality of Life

Whatever crossroads we come to in life, the higher analytical thinking of the sixth chakra will provide the best possible direction. Thinking from the mountaintop perspective of chakra six allows us to see answers and solutions through our third chakra intuition that go beyond our own personal attachments to our ego, body, and community to incorporate truths.

In Summary

- The sixth chakra is also known as our third eye and is associated with our faculties of analysis and intuition.

CHAPTER SIX: THE CHAKRA SIX CONNECTION – ANALYSIS AND INTUITION

- Rational analysis is an important foundation in decision making.
- The best decisions are those that incorporate rational analysis and intuitive perception.
- Human intuition is a gift that all humans have but use in varying degrees.
- Intuition is a capability that grows and improves through mediation.
- Sixth chakra intuition is our ability to directly perceive information.

THE 7 CONNECTIONS TO HAPPINESS AND HARMONY

Chapter Seven

The Crown Chakra Connection
Vision and Higher Purpose

Defining the Seventh Chakra

The crown chakra, signified by the thousand-petal lotus, helps us build a stronger sense of awareness of ourselves and the world around us. This chakra brings us knowledge, wisdom, understanding, and spiritual connection.

The word *crown* makes us think of a beautiful jewel-laden piece worn on top of the head; just as with the crown chakra, such a beautiful piece figuratively adorns that important region of the body. The crown chakra is located at the top of the head and is our connection to the greater world beyond, the merger of our unique souls into the divine realm of the universe.

The seventh chakra is not fully awakened or active in most humans. The seventh chakra is associated with reaching the highest levels of spiritual enlightenment, liberation, or nirvana and is experienced by the most enlightened souls and saints across religions.

THE 7 CONNECTIONS TO HAPPINESS AND HARMONY

Chakra Seven

Location:
Top of the Head

Sanskrit Name:
Sahasrara

Color: Violet [26]

Spiritual Evolution

As I talk about the crown chakra being the ultimate state of bliss or nirvana, it is valuable to understand the path or evolutionary process for reaching that ultimate state. The eastern Yogis believe that as immortal souls, with each life and each experience we are evolving.

Swami Kriyanada speaks about life that evolves upward from levels lower even than apparent movement. He points out that the wriggling worm, relatively high on the scale of consciousness, may next become a moth, then a bird, a mammal, and, after a long upward journey, a human being.[27]

Awakening the crown chakra signifies a final stage in a soul's evolution and signals the liberation of the soul from the imprisonment of the physical body that it occupies. The seventh chakra is not awakened in most humans. However,

Chapter Seven: The Crown Chakra Connection – Vision and Higher Purpose

what is awakened is a natural pull and curiosity toward a higher vision or higher truth.

In the Introduction, I spoke of how the human life force energy moves like a two-way current (upward and downward) through two channel passageways. I spoke of these corresponding to two completely opposing outlooks or pulls in our thinking — one is in the direction of expansion (in being open to information, people, ideas) and the opposite being that of *contraction* (in limiting information, reducing options, defining scope). Chakra seven epitomizes the upward pull of energy. Chakra seven leads us to an expanded state of intelligence, bliss, happiness, truth, freedom, and much more.

Discussion of chakra seven is with the full understanding that not all people are able to embrace the ideas and thinking associated with chakra seven. For those who are struggling for daily sustenance, there is very little time and, therefore, limited interest in seeking higher truths or a greater spiritual understanding. In today's modern fast-paced society, there is much stress, and limited time that can be spent on focusing on higher truths. Most people stay bogged down addressing and fulfilling the needs in their lower chakras. As a result, thinking and pursuing these topics can feel like a luxury. In India, seeking higher truths is often best left to the later stages of life once one's family duties are taken care of.

At different stages of life, we have different priorities based on our past experiences or current circumstances. The Yogis teach that at one point, the pleasures we seek will become "old hat" and we will reach a point where we will look to something greater for fulfillment.

The Upward Pull of Chakra Seven

While most humans do not have an awakened seventh chakra, for our discussion, I refer to chakra seven as the chakra for seeking higher purposes.

- **Seeking Wisdom** — Understanding the world around us more fully and seeing a total panorama of thought with all the dots connected at once.

THE 7 CONNECTIONS TO HAPPINESS AND HARMONY

- **Seeking Greater Meaning** — Looking for a greater purpose or greater fulfillment in one's life. This greater meaning is one that extends beyond the need for making money or achieving material success.

- **Seeking Spiritual Connections** — Developing a deeper connection to spirit through one's faith or spiritual practices.

- **Seeking Happiness for Others** — Seeking happiness for others as an integral part of one's own happiness.

Inspirational Stories

Some of the most noteworthy, accomplished individuals are those who focus on seeking a higher purpose for the world. As we look at Nobel laureates, their contributions further the knowledge of society as a whole. For artists and other highly accomplished individuals, seeking a higher purpose is paramount to the way they lead their lives.

When rock singer Bono of the band U2 visited Ethiopia during a famine, he realized a larger purpose for himself. An egoist might have seen the suffering and deprivation and beat a hasty retreat, justifying himself that the situation had nothing at all to do with him. Bono, on the other hand, commented, "In Ethiopia during the famine, I saw stuff there that reorganized how I saw the world. I didn't quite know what to do about it. At a certain point, I felt God is not looking for alms. God is looking for action." [28] This higher vision prompted Bono to organize relief efforts for the starving people of Ethiopia.

Bill Gates is another example of someone who works in accordance of a higher purpose. In his commencement address to Harvard University class of 2007, he shared this perspective when he said, "Humanity's greatest advances are not in its discoveries — but in how those discoveries are applied to reduce

CHAPTER SEVEN: THE CROWN CHAKRA CONNECTION – VISION AND HIGHER PURPOSE

inequity. Whether through democracy, strong public education, quality health care, or broad economic opportunity — reducing inequity is the highest human achievement." The Bill and Melinda Gates Foundation focuses on bringing innovations in health and learning to the global economy.

Former Vice President Al Gore passionately pursues his higher purpose through his work in global climate change. His political reputation and connections became tools he could use to promote understanding for an urgent cause. As a former vice president, he might have espoused many issues and causes that were self-aggrandizing and that gave him the personal spotlight. Yet he utilized the attention he received from his Nobel Peace Prize to warn that global warming is, "the greatest challenge we've ever faced."

Seeking Our Own Personal Vision

As we look at these examples, we see that the impact and momentum they have generated has been significant. But on a more personal note for these men, what is also striking is the amount of passion and conviction that motivated them. It's easy to dismiss the relevance of these examples by saying, "Once I am a rock star or a billionaire or a former vice president of the United States, I can think about addressing my passions!" However, I have a very opposite view. We should not have to wait until we are famous or rich to be able to find passion or inner fulfillment. Finding passion is at the crux of mountaintop thinking.

Is there a particular passion that you would like to explore or pursue?

_____
_____
_____
_____

THE 7 CONNECTIONS TO HAPPINESS AND HARMONY

Seeking a Mountaintop Vision

Chakra six and our ascent into chakra seven symbolize our final destination into mountaintop thinking. From the mountaintop, we have the vantage point to see the world around us while remaining intimately aware of all the influences, stresses, and inclinations felt across the other chakras. This elevated thinking gives us the inner calmness to make intelligent, wise, and rational decisions. In Chapter One, we talked about the root chakra as being a chakra of base instincts and a chakra focused on more reactive decisions. The mountaintop perspective provides the completely opposite perspective as being the chakra of proactive thinking.

Chakra seven allows us to think beyond base safety, beyond excitement, beyond our personal egos, beyond our lower chakras to find the right decisions. Through the vantage point of standing at the top of the mountain, we are in a unique position to define our destiny. Or, in other words, we are in a position to create and be guided by our own unique vision. The results of creating a vision can be powerful and truly empowering.

The Importance of Vision

As I look at individuals who are unhappy with certain aspects in their lives or organizations that are underperforming, it is evident that there is something fundamentally broken in the vision. When we are operating in the absence of a vision, the symptoms can be that we are running ourselves ragged, we are tired, or that life feels fragmented, with many moving parts that do not make sense. In other cases, we can feel like we are sleepwalking through life.

The good news is that these kinds of feelings are usually temporary. Either something changes in our environment or something changes in our own thinking that eventually frees us from some of this unhappy cycle. The other good news is that things can become clearer and more rewarding through our own efforts. Creating a vision is also a very simple process, which is broken down into five steps.

CHAPTER SEVEN: THE CROWN CHAKRA CONNECTION – VISION AND HIGHER PURPOSE

STEP #1:
Thinking Begins with a Vision

In my experiences with coaching and mentoring professionals, my favorite exercise is a visualization exercise. If you were filming a movie about yourself in the future, how would the setting look, and how would you fit into that movie? Think about how you would feel and the types of emotions you are experiencing. As simplistic as this visioning exercise may seem, it helps us create a multidimensional vision of the future we want.

Visualization techniques also work effectively in the professional environment as you envision the type of future you see for your organization. While the goals and responsibilities are different, it fundamentally comes down to creating this multi-dimensional picture of the future.

STEP #2:
Define Your Practical Needs

In building our vision, we must understand and embrace our practical needs and create a vision for how we want to see our practical needs being fulfilled. The practical is largely tied to our financial needs, social needs, values, health, and the needs of our immediate family. Our practical requirements generally correlate to our base chakras. For example, our practical side might encompass a plan to save a certain amount of money for retirement. This practical dimension may encourage us to lead a healthy lifestyle through proper diet and exercise. This practical

bent to vision is not limited to our personal life. In fact, organizations are adept at building structured processes to address the practical reporting functions such as revenues, profits, efficiencies, and even head count.

STEP #3:
Embrace Your Personal Passion

While our practical needs are important, our souls crave deeper fulfillment. This fulfillment may be through hobbies and activities or finding a higher purpose or calling. These could be creative pursuits such as painting or gardening, learning new subjects, or working on a higher cause such as poverty or global warming. Yogis and the devoutly religious may increasingly feel a need to move to a more spiritually centered life. While it may be easy to be enticed by so many interests or hobbies, a personal vision is about focusing on the areas you feel the most passionate about.

In the ideal scenario, we can work in a career or profession that we love. However, this may not always be practical or possible. For instance, with a young, growing family of five, a career as an amateur violinist may not put food on the table! Nevertheless, if we lead lives that are missing inner excitement or passion, we ultimately become tired and emotionally depleted. It is in these situations, when our professional lives are less aligned with our passions, that we must bring these interests and hobbies into our lives.

STEP #4:
Expand Your Vision

So far, we have spoken about the two necessary dimensions of our vision — the practical and the personal. There is another aspect to creating a vision that can greatly increase our level of fulfillment. This is when we start to think about our vision in relation to a higher purpose, a higher cause. In other words, thinking about our vision in relation to helping others and including others in our happiness and success.

CHAPTER SEVEN: THE CROWN CHAKRA CONNECTION – VISION AND HIGHER PURPOSE

There is a trend toward social responsibility where corporations donate a portion of profits to selected charities. Other companies have matching programs that encourage employees to contribute to charities with an added corporate support system. In our lives, it comes naturally to help those who are closest to us. But as we start to think about creating a vision and set of values that are aligned with helping people who may not be in our immediate circle, our capacity for love expands and so does our capacity for happiness.

STEP #5:
Articulate and Empower Others with Your Vision

Once you have created this personal vision for yourself, the exciting part is articulating this vision to others. When the vision is the right one and delivered effectively, it will resonate and connect with its stakeholders. In my observation, the significant obstacle that leaders face is the ability to define and articulate a vision. It is very easy to spot those leaders whose messages feel like alphabet soup rather than a tightly articulated plan or idea. But there are leaders that come few and far between who have the ability to inspire masses.

Personal Example as a Former FedEx Employee

Early in my career, I had the good fortune of working for one of the most visionary corporate environments of our time. While working for FedEx Corporation, I, like literally all the employees, deeply believed that CEO Fred Smith provided a level of vision that was many years ahead of the marketplace. The speeches he delivered inspired all employees. It became a common expression among the employees of the company to begin comments by saying, "Fred says..." There was so much pride in the mission of FedEx. We heard all the wonderful stories of saving lives and transporting hearts, as well as all the interesting stories of transporting horses and cattle. One of the most classic examples of FedEx and its higher mission occurred over the Christmas holidays, when FedEx requested all of its employees (from the execs in the ivory tower, to the engineers, to

The 7 Connections to Happiness and Harmony

the scientists, to the marketing departments) to work in the hub, helping meet the deadlines in the holiday rush. This sort of teamwork, pride, and camaraderie is a testimony to the ability of FedEx to inspire and create a higher vision for its employees.

Blockages

Through organizations like FedEx, we can see how a vision can move individuals and groups forward. However, it is easy to fall into certain blockages and pitfalls on our way to seeking a higher vision.

Blockage #1:
Extremism

The connection that humans have to seeking a higher purpose can be powerful and potentially dangerous when they become misguided in their purpose. This can lead to a tunnel vision, where we are so focused on our one way of looking at the world that we ignore other perspectives and lose sight of our morals, wisdom, and better judgment. In the history of humans there has always been a struggle between religions. At the extreme case, this can lead to some disturbing questions. We look at suicide bombers and terrorists who have no consideration for their own lives, let alone the lives of others. In theory, they believe that they are sacrificing for something greater. To others outside their religiously held beliefs, the view is considerably different. The ideology or leader of one group clashes with that of another.

Swami Kriyananda discusses this very important topic of religious conflict. He explains that while there have been "wars and persecutions in the name of God, these must be blamed on human nature, not on teachings that tell them to love God and to be at peace with one another. People all too easily infect one another with their own imperfections." [29]

While these clashes can be significant, there is one overall approach to mountaintop thinking that may help. As we begin

CHAPTER SEVEN: THE CROWN CHAKRA CONNECTION – VISION AND HIGHER PURPOSE

to feel that our vision is actually pulling us downward toward divisiveness and negativity, we should think about finding ways to broaden our understanding and find ways to apply our vision in a broader context. This involves an additive mindset that allows us to look at the points that are in common.

An expansive mindset means working with others who have conflicting perspectives and finding common areas of understanding, whether we speak about a business, a social organization, or a family. As you apply this expansive mindset to creating or refining your vision, you will find new ways of doing things and a deeper, richer understanding of the subject matter.

BLOCKAGE #2:
Vision Without Action

As we operate from this higher vantage point or vision, we can become very good at thinking and coming up with ideas and vision. However, we can falter when we are unable to convert our higher vision into practical and tangible results. In the business world, there are many brilliant and articulate strategists who are unable to deliver results. And I have seen the opposite with highly effective tacticians who focused on the efficiency and implementations of actions without looking at the larger picture.

As I relate this back to the seven chakras, it's quite intuitive to see that certain roles by design require the use of certain chakras. A tactical line manager role will require the use of the lower chakras that are heavily geared to tangible actions. CEOs and executives, who are less intimately familiar with the operations, will rely on their intuition and higher chakras to navigate their daily decision making.

In addressing this blockage, I believe that the best strategists are those that have a unique multi-lens, mountaintop perspective. This is a perspective that allows us to see with both a telescope and microscope. A telescope is to see the larger vision, while a microscope allows us to understand the tactical requirements for implementing an idea.

The 7 Connections to Happiness and Harmony

Having both views means maintaining a calm, detached, intuitive disposition while also staying grounded and connected to the people and activities in your organization. This not only keeps us more aware of the practical realities of the vision we create, it also keeps us more humble, and part of the team that is actually contributing to the vision. Whether this is a CEO who is creating a vision for a company or a parent in the PTA who is planning activities for their child's elementary school, staying connected with the hub of activity ensures that the vision that is created can be attainable.

Secrets in Mountaintop Thinking

As we stand on the mountaintop, there are two final secrets to share.

▲▲ SECRET #1:
Understanding the Role of Faith in Your Decision Making

The seventh chakra is the chakra that is heavily connected to our inner yearning for spiritual fulfillment. Each person has a unique relationship with faith in a higher spirit. The Yogic perspective of faith is that it should develop through personal experience. Belief may sprout from an intuitive perception or from one's environment and training. Over time, that faith should strengthen and inwardly grow as the individual feels the presence of a higher spirit.

The truth is that while we should not judge others, we should realize that one's views on faith are an important lens through which they look at the world. Simply put, our relation to faith influences how we see the world. And as we make decisions and understand the decision making of others, it is important to take this into consideration.

▲▲ SECRET #2:
Develop Detachment

The final secret to mountaintop thinking is to be as detached as possible from the final outcome that you are

CHAPTER SEVEN: THE CROWN CHAKRA CONNECTION – VISION AND HIGHER PURPOSE

striving for. The concept of detachment is a fundamental principle in Yogic thinking. By being detached from results, we are in a position to have more calmness and clarity in the decisions we make and the actions we complete.

By making choices and decisions in accordance with what resonates, you hopefully have the energy and passion to make sure that you are using your maximum effort toward right decisions and right actions. However, once a decision is made, it is important to maintain a level of detachment from the actual results. We should use our intellect and our hard work in putting forward our strongest effort. But when all is said and done, we should let the chips fall where they may land.

Detachment does not mean indifference to suffering. On the contrary, detachment to the result allows for greater focus, commitment and resolve in addressing the suffering. It takes inner strength to let certain worries go. Learn how to let the world and its challenges wipe off your body, just as water drips off of a swan.

In Summary

- The seventh chakra is called the crown chakra and is considered the final in the set of seven chakras.

- For most human beings, the seventh chakra is not awakened. It only becomes awakened through advanced spiritual practices such as meditation.

- While most humans do not have an awakened seventh chakra, they do have the tendency and capacity to seek a higher purpose and meaning.

- Creating a vision in one's personal or professional life is both a powerful tool and an important factor in one's success.

 **THE 7 CONNECTIONS TO HAPPINESS AND HARMONY**

Chapter Eight

Bringing It All Together

The Free Will of Great Decisions

The journey of life is one of joy and one of endless decisions. Each day we are bombarded with numerous decisions and choices. Sometimes, these decisions can seem so complex that we wish we didn't have to make them. I see this with my family and friends battling cancer and making important choices in treatment. As they evaluate treatment options, they find that none of the choices are simple. Each choice has its related side effects and consequences, making the decision process so challenging.

But then I also think about the parts of the world where the women are powerless in their families and in their communities. And they are unable to stand on their own and make their own decisions. And then I realize how valuable and what a privilege it is to have choices.

While some of our most important decisions can make us feel anxious or unsure, these choices are also very empowering. A decision is a way to exercise our fundamental free will as human beings. This free will allows us to advance ourselves further in our personal, professional, and spiritual lives.

Self-Awareness:
The Key to Sound Decisions

The topic of decision making is a broad one for which there is no one-size-fits-all model. Approaches can vary considerably by culture, industry, and topic. A day trader may rely on an advanced financial or statistical model, while a bargain hunter may study the Sunday newspaper to find special deals.

Underneath the processes and the decision tools is a human person who navigates this information to make choices. For each person, sound decisions begin with better self-awareness. The Seven Chakras provide a valuable blueprint that facilitates self-discovery. Each chakra represents a set of thoughts, feelings, and behaviors that we experience but may not ever articulate.

The premise of my writing is that understanding how our inner thought machinery works can put us on a path for making fundamentally better decisions. In workshops, the chakra model helped to awaken a new level of self-awareness within my students. They began to really connect with emotions that were hidden underneath the surface — developing deeper clarity. Through the workshops, these students came to feel more comfortable and in a better position to make wise decisions.

In studying the seven chakras, I realized that our biggest decision-making pitfall and opportunity is when we act based on unfounded biases or blockages that inhibit the flow of ideas. The seven chakras can help us see areas where we are weak or have blockages. Each of the chapters walks through examples of proper, balanced use of each chakra as well as examples of blockages within each chakra. By understanding our own biases and limitations, we can seek out ways to restore balance in our decision process. This may mean bringing in other people who do not share the same blockage to help in the decision-making process, or it may mean confronting your bias head-on, as in the case of fear blockage.

Chapter Eight: Bringing It All Together

> *When the world goes flat — and you are feeling flattened — reach for a shovel inside yourself. Don't try to build walls.*[30]
> — *Thomas L. Friedman*

In this rapidly globalizing marketplace, now more than ever it is important to establish a mindset and attitude that is receptive and understanding of different cultures. Thomas Friedman shares his insights on globalization and the future of the global workforce in his book *The World Is Flat*. His reference to the word flat is in terms of commerce and competition, as in a level playing field — one where all competitors have an equal opportunity. He advises readers that those who can navigate in a globalizing workforce will be successful.

His book sends a brilliant message about the need to think more globally. But the paradigm shift is one that requires facing and overcoming blockages that one may have. There is a natural sense of familiarity that each of us has with our own culture. But the most successful people in this new world will be those who can move beyond their own biases and blockages and think about the common values, ideas, and friendships that can be shared with people from differing cultures. By understanding and confronting these biases, one will be ready to handle them as they happen.

The fundamental principle of decision-making through the seven chakras is that for our best decisions, we want to access a wide assortment of information from across all our chakras. And we want to have an open flow of energy across all chakras without any blockages in a particular chakra. The mountaintop mindset exemplifies this model of elevated thinking. The open flow of energy across all our chakras facilitates a natural flow of information. And the more open and receptive we are to information, the greater ability we have to make smarter, wiser, and better decisions.

The chakra blueprint does another very exciting thing. It allows us to see our potential and start to awaken certain powerful

faculties that we may not realize we have. For example, many people do not realize that they have certain intuitive gifts that can be developed and strengthened over time. The seven chakras give us this X-ray into ourselves to find areas for expansion and improvement.

The Seven Chakras as a Decision Framework

In addition to using the seven chakras as a tool for personal self-awareness, we can apply them as a stand-alone model for structured discussions. The Appendix includes a framework and sequence of steps that can guide individuals or groups in evaluating a decision. The Appendix outlines a decision framework.

Values and Priorities

The aim of a structured model for decision making is to guide us toward isolating the values and priorities which are the most critical and urgent. Once the key issues are isolated, we can begin the difficult process of making the important choices and trade-offs between different priorities.

Decisions, by definition, are the choice between two or more competing options. Certain trade-offs might be timeline based, short-term versus long-term. For example, when making the choice to attend a four-year college, someone is choosing to forgo a salary in favor of having a better career after four years. We can also experience trade-offs with different criteria and priorities. For example, when we are interviewing candidates for a job, we may face a choice between a candidate whose personality is a better fit for the organization and a candidate whose resume is a better fit for the role.

The seven chakras provide a blueprint that allows us to parse out the factors at play to balance our practical needs for financial stability and safety with personal needs of happiness and fulfillment.

We Own Our Decisions

Another important factor in decision making are those individuals in our lives who influence us. The environment in which we live and the people who surround us can play a crucial role influencing our choices.

At the end of the day, while others may bully us or be persuasive, decisions are personal choices with personal consequences. When we are stuck at an important crossroads, it is easy to lose sight of this. For example, a real estate agent may encourage a client to pay more to purchase a home, but it is the buyer who pays the mortgage and takes on the risk. In certain decisions, such as in the case of purchasing a home, we can feel the direct consequence. However, even in cases where we do not feel the immediate consequences of our actions, we own our decisions. While others can guide us or manipulate or bully us toward a particular decision, each of us has the responsibility to make the best possible decision that resonates with us.

Decisions with Heart

Our heart chakra plays a crucial role in our decision making. When our heart is not in the decision, it is very hard to be decisive and muster up the courage to move forward. If someone interviews for a job and doesn't have the right comfort level with the company or people, he or she may end up taking the job but may hesitate before signing on.

The heart, being the central point of convergence and the feeling center for all our chakras, is our special tool for guiding us toward decisions that feel right. The top sheaths of heart chakra are more visceral emotions — tied to our lower chakra instinctive senses. Layer by layer, as we open our hearts, we are enabled to feel more and more. As we start to develop our heart chakra, we start to open up our capacity to love. This love allows us to make decisions that are more compassionate. And this love also allows us to see opportunities for making decisions that can lead to an overall better result.

Given the power of the heart chakra, the challenge we can find ourselves in is that our emotions are so strong that our judgment

can be clouded. We lose objectivity and lose touch with the truth that is masked by our heart chakra. This leads us toward a need for balanced decision making.

Good Decisions are Balanced Decisions

Given the powerful nature of the heart, the question we must ask is: How do we best use the heart in decision making? In the academic arena, there is a focus on analytical rigor and scientific methods in order to help limit human bias. However, this focus on eliminating or reducing the role of the heart does not allow us to embrace the unique qualities of the heart. In my research into decision making, I came to understand that the best decisions are those that balance emotions of the heart with rational thinking and wisdom from the head. *The Art of War* was compiled over 2,000 years ago by a mysterious warrior and philosopher, Sun Tzu. Today it is considered one of the most influential books on strategy. He says that "leadership is a matter of intelligence, trustworthiness, humaneness, courage and sternness."

An interpretation of this by Du Mu states:

> *The way of the ancient kings was to consider humaneness foremost, while the martial artists considered intelligence foremost. This is because intelligence involves the ability to plan and to know when to change effectively. Trustworthiness means to make people sure of punishment or reward. Humaneness means love and compassion for people, being aware of their toils. Courage means to seize opportunities to make certain of victory, without vacillation. Sternness means to establish discipline in the ranks by strict punishments.*[31]

While the conflict that Sun Tzu speaks of takes place on a physical battlefield, each of us has an inner battlefield of our consciousness, where we are continually reconciling and balancing different priorities. Our best decisions are those that take the best of all seven chakras. Understanding and using these capabilities in a balanced way is the ultimate secret to mountaintop thinking.

Decisions that Resonate

Ultimately, I believe that our best decisions are those that not only balance the needs and energies we have across multiple chakras, but also resonate deeply. These are the choices we feel passionate about. Our vision may be a practical one, such as making a good life for one's family. Or the vision may extend to encompass others and a more lofty goal. Whatever the choice is, the right one is the choice that personally resonates.

In my study of the seven chakras, I have developed a deeper and richer love for the soul qualities of humans. At the core of all human beings is the need for honesty and truth. In my view, the choices we make should ultimately strike a chord with the truth that resonates with us.

When confronted with a challenging decision, it's clear that the choices are rarely cut and dry. This is because we are making choices in an environment that is imperfect and there are many unknown variables. But if you can align your decision-making process to focus on making choices that feel true, honest, and right, that also fit the vision that you see for your life while addressing compassion and the needs of others — those are the wisest decisions.

Final Personal Note

My personal experience with the seven chakras has been one of great personal awakening. I initially started on this journey to guide me in my professional pursuits in marketing. It is hard to place a price tag on self-awareness or self-reflection. But through this process, I realized that power of the human potential. And

THE 7 CONNECTIONS TO HAPPINESS AND HARMONY

collectively, as each of us strive to use our hearts and higher intuitive faculties, we can make decisions that not only maximize our material successes but also lead us toward finding better answers that benefit all people.

Good luck in all your future decision-making endeavors!

Shirley Desai

APPENDIX

Seven Chakras Decision Framework Worksheet

STEP 1:
Problem Definition.

The first step of any important decision process is to properly frame the problem, issue or decision at hand. The more carefully you scope out your problem, the better your decision becomes. Think about the problem on rational terms and emotional terms.

State the problem or issue that you are considering. Are there any choices or options you might consider?

_____

_____

_____

Are there any other factors to consider about the decision? (Environment, timeline, past experiences, decision makers)

_____

_____

_____

STEP 2:
Analyze and determine all the important factors in your decision. Document the factors that relate to the first six chakras:

Chakra 1: Root Chakra

- How important is safety or familiarity in this choice?
  _____

- Which choice feels the safest?
  _____

THE 7 CONNECTIONS TO HAPPINESS AND HARMONY

Seven Chakras Decision Framework Worksheet

- What are the risks? (*Risks of each option, opportunity costs of choosing one option over another option*)

  _____

- Do you feel anxiety or fear?

  _____

Chakra 2: Excitement and Pleasure

- How does excitement fit into this choice?

  _____

- Are any of your options exciting or interesting?

  _____

- Is this the right time to make a change or a decision?

  _____

- Is there something exciting or positive that can result from any of the decisions?

  _____

Chakra 3: Ego, Values, Principles

- What are the related values or principles that are important to you?

  _____

- How does this decision impact your reputation, the reputation of your organization, or the reputation of any other group that this decision relates to?

  _____

APPENDIX

Seven Chakras Decision Framework Worksheet

- Are there any special rules of thumb that help you in making decisions?

  _____

Chakra 4: Heart

- Are there any relationships involved in this decision?

  _____

- Is there a particular choice or aspect that you feel passionate about?

  _____

- What is your heart telling you about this decision?

  _____

Chakra 5: Creativity and Self-Expression

- Do you have a way to contribute creatively in making this choice or decision?

  _____

- Is creativity or self-expression an important factor of the decision?

  _____

- Does this decision allow you to express yourself in a unique or special way?

  _____

Chakra 6:

- Are there particular facts, data, heuristics that you relate to this choice?

  _____

THE 7 CONNECTIONS TO HAPPINESS AND HARMONY

Seven Chakras Decision Framework Worksheet

- Are there any trends or wider patterns that relate to this decision?

  _____

- Does your intuition (third eye) offer any additional insight?

  _____

Chakra 7:

- Does this decision, issue, choice relate to a plan, vision that you have already? If so, what is that vision?

  _____

STEP 3:
Prioritize the factors and values of importance.

The next step is to isolate the aspects of the decision that are the most critical. You can do this by putting a star next to the chakras or the related questions within each of the chakras in **Step 2** that are important factors in your decision.

STEP 4:
Reflect on past decisions.

Reflect on decisions that have gone well and decisions that have gone poorly. Think about any relevant lessons or rules of thumb that may apply to this decision.

_____
_____
_____
_____
_____

APPENDIX

Seven Chakras Decision Framework Worksheet

STEP 5:
Determine if you are ready to decide.

Are you ready to decide now, or do you need more time? If you need more time, when would you be ready to make this determination? What kinds of additional information would you like to find out?

_____
_____
_____
_____
_____

STEP 6:
Visualize the outcome you want.

Visualize the type of outcome you would ultimately like to have. Think about this vision in terms of addressing the practical needs you have in the decision as well as the personal needs you may also experience or enjoy with this outcome.

_____
_____
_____
_____
_____

STEP 7:
Decide whether you are ready to move forward with a decision.

_____
_____
_____
_____
_____

Seven Chakras Decision Framework Worksheet

STEP 8:
What is your decision?

_____
_____
_____
_____
_____

STEP 9:
What are your timelines, resource plans, and success metrics?

_____
_____
_____
_____
_____
_____
_____
_____
_____
_____
_____

STEP 10:

*Congratulate Yourself
on Making a
Seven Chakra Decision!!!*

Acknowledgements

The journey of writing a book has been one of my most enriching and spiritually uplifting experiences. There are many people who have helped me create this first book.

First, my husband, Apurva, who stood by me with tireless devotion, support, and patience as I wrote this book. He believed in me and in the truth that resides in the chakra system. I am eternally grateful.

I would like to thank the rest of my family and my wonderful support system of friends. My grandfather, Chandrasekhar Rao Vamaraju, has been a beacon of inspiration and a role model with his book on the Upanishads. Thanks especially to my brother-in-law, Sunil, for sharing his spiritual wisdom with me over many, many years. My dear friends, Valerie, Afsana, and Neeta, were the first readers of my full manuscript and provided thoughtful and incisive feedback. And my brilliant friend, Edward, has advised me and helped me understand the maze called publishing.

I must give special thanks to my editor, James Hamilton. His patience, professionalism, and support are deeply appreciated. Others include my copy editor, Kristin Kearns, and designers, Darlene Dion and Lewis Agrell.

I would like to acknowledge the gifted cartoonists J.C. Duffy, Randy Glasbergen, Mike Peters and Bob Thaves. It is an honor to include their work in my book.

Finally, it would be remiss of me to not thank the ultimate giver and source of all of the individuals named above.

THE 7 CONNECTIONS TO HAPPINESS AND HARMONY

REFERENCES

1. Anodea Judith, *Eastern Body Western Mind, Psychology and the Chakra System as a Path to the Self*, 2004, Celestial Arts, pages 4-6

2. Anodea Judith, *Eastern Body Western Mind, Psychology and the Chakra System as a Path to the Self*, 2004, Celestial Arts, page 6

3. Janet A. Simons, Donald B. Irwin, Beverly A. Drinnien, *Psychology — The Search for Understanding*, 1987, West Publishing Company, excerpt featured on website http://honolulu.hawaii.edu/intranet/committees/FacDevCom/guidebk/teachtip/maslow.htm

4. Maruti Seidman, *Balancing the Chakras*, 2000, North Atlantic Books, page 34

5. Neil F., Neimark, M.D. "The Fight or Flight Response", The Body/Soul Connection. February 2, 2009. http://www.thebodysoulconnection.com/EducationCenter/fight.html

6. Paramahansa Yogananda, *Living Fearlessly, Bringing Out Your Inner Soul Strength*, 2003, Self-Realization Fellowship, pages 15-18

7. Maruti Seidman, *Balancing the Chakras*, 2000, North Atlantic Books, page 39

8. Harish Johari, Chakras, *Energy Centers of Transformation*, Destiny Books, 2000, page 103

THE 7 CONNECTIONS TO HAPPINESS AND HARMONY

9   Dr. Elaine Aron. "A letter from Elaine Aron."
    <u>The Highly Sensitive Person</u>. February 2, 2009.
    http://www.hsperson.com/pages/hsp.htm

10 Martin E. P. Seligman, Ph.D., *Authentic Happiness, Using the New Positive Psychology to Realize Your Potential for Lasting Fulfillment*, 2002, Free Press, pages 102-105

11 Martin E. P. Seligman, Ph.D., *Authentic Happiness, Using the New Positive Psychology to Realize Your Potential for Lasting Fulfillment*, 2002, Free Press, page 113

12 Maruti Seidman, *Balancing the Chakras*, 2000, North Atlantic Books, page 45

13 "Ego." *The American Heritage® Dictionary of the English Language, Fourth Edition.* Houghton Mifflin Company, 2004. 13 July 2009. Dictionary.com http://dictionary.reference.com/browse/ego

14 "Colin Powell Quotes." Thinkexist.com. Feb 2, 2009. http://en.thinkexist.com/quotes/colin_powell/2.html

15 Gerd Gigerenzer, Gut Feelings, *The Intelligence of the Unconscious*, 2007, Viking, pages 16-19

16 "Anahata." Wikipedia: The Free Encyclopedia. February 2, 2009. http://en.wikipedia.org/wiki/Anahata

17 Maruti Seidman, *Balancing the Chakras*, 2000, North Atlantic Books, page 50

18 Joan Guntzelman, *A Retreat With Mother Teresa and Damien of Molokai: Caring for Those Who Suffer*, 1999, Saint Anthony Messenger Press, Quote featured on excerpt. http://www.americancatholic.org/features/teresa/WhoWasTeresa.asp

References

19 "MySpace." Wikipedia: The Free Encyclopedia. February 2, 2009. http://en.wikipedia.org/wiki/MySpace

20 Maruti Seidman, *Balancing the Chakras*, 2000, North Atlantic Books, page 56

21 Jeanette Walls, *The Glass Castle*, 2005, Scribner

22 Bill Breen, "The 6 Myths of Creativity," Fast Company Magazine, Issue 89, December 2004, page 75

23 Maruti Seidman, *Balancing the Chakras*, 2000, North Atlantic Books, page 61

24 Anodea Judith, page 357

25 Anodea Judith, page 357

26 Maruti Seidman, *Balancing the Chakras*, 2000, North Atlantic Books, page 66

27 *The Essence of the Bhagavad Gita*, Explained by Paramanhansa Yogananda remembered by Swami Kriyananda, 2006, Crystal Clarity Publishers, Nevada City, CA, page 136

28 Bono, Oprah Winfrey Show, 2002. http://www.quotationspage.com/quote/38173.html

29 *The Essence of the Bhagavad Gita*, Explained by Paramanhansa Yoganand remembered by Swami Kriyananda, 2006, Crystal Clarity Publishers, Nevada City, CA, page 157

30 Thomas L. Friedman, *The World is Flat — A Brief History of The Twenty-First Century*, 2005, 2006, Farrar Straus and Giroux Books, page 426

31 Sun Tzu, Translated by Thomas Cleary, *The Art of War*, 1988, Shambhala Publications, page 45

www.ingramcontent.com/pod-product-compliance
Lightning Source LLC
Chambersburg PA
CBHW072336300426
44109CB00042B/1641